Mel STERLAND

Boozing
Betting
&
Brawling

Mel STERLAND

A FOOTBALLERS LIFE
With **Nick JOHNSON**

Boozing Betting & Brawling

Foreword by
Howard WILKINSON

Green**Umbrella**
Publishing

This edition first published in the UK in 2008
By Green Umbrella Publishing

© Green Umbrella Publishing 2008

www.gupublishing.co.uk

Publishers: Jules Gammond and Vanessa Gardner

Creative Director: Kevin Gardner

Picture Credits: Getty Images and Mel Sterland

Printed and bound by J. H. Haynes & Co. Ltd., Sparkford

ISBN: 978-1-906229-70-2

I would like to dedicate this book to my wife Charmaine, who is my soul-mate and the love of my life. It is also dedicated to my children, Chantelle and Nathan, who I am so proud of. And to my grandson Leon, who's a star. Not forgetting my late Mum and Dad because without them, none of my achievements would have been possible. God Bless.

Contents

Mel STERLAND

Foreword

If you've known Mel as long as I have, you'll know there's never a dull moment when he's around; this book is no different. From good to bad, happy to suicidal, success to abject failure and wealth to poverty: a roller-coaster in every sense of the word.

One thing Mel's life has never been, however, is boring. During the whole of that topsy-turvy journey, he's always managed to retain his ability to be liked. Indeed, when he was on the verge of retiring, due to injury at Leeds United, skipper Gordon Strachan organised a collection from the players and staff, in order to mark his departure from the club. When Gordon told me the total amount he had collected, he was truly overwhelmed. He said that never in the whole of his long career had he experienced such a response. Not one person at the club had shown anything but the utmost generosity and willingness to contribute.

Boozing, Betting & Brawling

To the outside world, Mel was and is the eternal optimist, always happy, smiling and generous to a fault. There is, however, a darker side to Mel, which I experienced when we were together at Sheffield Wednesday. Late one Thursday afternoon, Alan Smith, the physio, knocked on my office door and suggested I go down to the treatment room. I did so and found Mel, lying on a couch, with a towel over his head and shaking uncontrollably. He was convinced he had cancer. I frantically arranged a series of consultations with specialists and it was not until the Saturday morning that we were able to confirm that all the tests were clear. Mel played that afternoon as if nothing had ever happened.

Other deep sources of worry were also eating away at him. I found out he had serious money problems and I became a counter-signatory on all his cheques in order to try and put some control on his spending. I have to say that I had no suspicion at that time of the serious gambling or drink problems that were to later emerge as further complications in his life. Around the time I realised the extent of his problems and started dealing with them, I left Sheffield Wednesday to join Leeds United and Mel moved up to Glasgow Rangers soon afterwards.

The rest, as they say, is now history. History, in his words, documented as he saw it and that darker side has, to a degree, won the day. It is a story, unfortunately, all too common in football and, I suspect, in other sports. Fortunately, the problems Mel encountered occur less and less these days because there are mechanisms in place to deal with them, ensuring the demons don't win.

Mel STERLAND

In his time, Mel was the most popular athlete in South Yorkshire. Everybody was his friend and he played the part, with respect and generosity, giving both his time and money in equal amounts. He has given pleasure and put smiles on the faces of thousands of people, especially at a time when his performances were the highlight of the week for many of those striking South Yorkshire miners and their families.

Mel's life reads like a novel, but it's fact, not fiction. In all the time he was with me, both at Sheffield Wednesday and Leeds United, he gave terrific value-for-money to his team, his team-mates and the public. He's also been a devoted husband to Charmaine and a good father to Chantelle and Nathan.

A final word: please be careful not to judge. As the Red Indians say, "Don't judge a man until you've walked a mile in his moccasins." Remember, this story started with an ordinary, working-class kid, born on a housing estate, who had all the physical talent in the world and who could have starred in any sport of his choosing. Here's hoping this book sees better times ahead for Mel.

Howard Wilkinson

May 2008

Acknowledgements

For their love and support, I am grateful to my brothers Glyn, John, Georgie, Terry and Malcolm and sisters Sheila, Avril and Sharon. Thanks to my in-laws: Sammy, Christine, Anthony, Christopher and Sarah along with their partners. There are also my various nephews and nieces, along with Godchildren Kymarni, Crystal, Luke and Rebecca.

I'd like to mention some close friends who've always been there for me and Charmaine, through good times and bad. They are Tom and Sandra Graham, Andy and Audrey Hobson, Geri and Paul Kellett, Janet and Phillip Knowles, Imre Varadi and Charlie and Louise Williamson.

I would also like to acknowledge Howard and Sam Wilkinson and the rest of the managers, players and backroom staff I was fortunate enough to work with in my career. They include Jack Charlton, Maurice Setters, Robin Wray,

Mel STERLAND

Albert Phelan, Mick Hennigan, Peter Eustace, Ron Atkinson, Alan Smith, Alan Sutton and Shaun Hardy. Not forgetting a trio from the early days: Doc Martin, Eric Gyte and Charlie Wain. For reminding me of some anecdotes, thanks go to Gordon Simmonite, David Grant and Mick Cunningham.

I am grateful to all my drinking friends and their partners who have stood by me (in the pub) on a Friday. They are Robert, Brian, Eddie, Jack, Malcolm, "Knighty", Martin, "Bash", Mark, "Twins", "Waggy", Gerald, "Daz" Manning, Matt, "Disco Daz", Tony Aziz, Andy Pearson, Chris and John.

Thanks to Steve Penistone and his staff for steering us in the right direction and I can't leave out "The Cutting Club": Michael, Ruth, Ian, Vanessa, Joanne, Zoe and Kay. Thanks also to Anne and Freddie Holt and family for all their support over the years.

I'd like to thank photographer Steve Parkin for taking the photo used on the front cover of the book and Dave Allen for allowing his casino – Napoleon's in Sheffield – to be used for the photo-shoot.

Vanessa Gardner and her staff at Green Umbrella Publishing deserve praise for the support and encouragement they have provided. Thanks also to Vanessa for believing in this book from the moment she read the synopsis.

Thanks finally to Nick Johnson for working with me on the book and putting it all together. We've had some laughs along the way and I'm delighted with the end result.

Introduction

My obsession with football began when I was a lad growing up in Sheffield during the late 70s and early 80s. Around the same time, Mel Sterland was beginning to make a name for himself in the game as a marauding full-back whose attacking style made him a hugely popular figure among Sheffield Wednesday fans.

Later, after a spell north of the border with Rangers – helping the Glasgow giants win the first of nine titles in a row – Mel returned to Yorkshire to join a Leeds side managed by his old Wednesday boss Howard Wilkinson. I was behind the goal when Mel beat Sheffield United keeper Simon Tracey with a superbly-struck free-kick at Bramall Lane in a season when Leeds won the Second Division title.

Leeds became the First Division champions the following season, making

Mel STERLAND

Mel one of only a handful of players to have won titles in both England and Scotland. Mel's career was sadly cut short by injury, but he achieved more than most during his time in the game and is fondly remembered by those who were fortunate enough to see him play.

When Mel began to get involved in media work on match days, I started seeing him regularly in the Press Box at Hillsborough and found him to be a friendly, approachable character, with a good sense of humour. All those I have spoken to who know Mel describe him in similar terms.

The idea for this book came about when I met up with Mel at a Sheffield hotel to interview him for a feature on *Sky Sports News*. We chatted as the cameraman I was working with was setting up for the interview and Mel told me about one or two incidents which took place during his playing career. I thought the anecdotes were hilarious and quickly came to the conclusion that the story of his life and career should be told.

Mel readily accepted my offer to help him write a book, agreeing to discuss every aspect of his life in detail. He was as good as his word and the result is a full and frank account. As well as chronicling the highs of a career which saw him win domestic honours and represent his country, the book also covers times in Mel's life when he has slumped to the depths of despair. He talks about drinking to excess, suffering life-threatening health problems and seriously contemplating suicide. Tales of fighting, gambling and being wrongly accused of handling stolen goods also feature, setting it apart from your average footballer's autobiography.

It has been a pleasure to work with Mel on this book and I hope you find the journey through his life as fascinating as I have.

Nick Johnson

May 2008

www.nickjohnson.tv

Mel STERLAND

CHAPTER ONE

"I'm Going To End It All"

I'd hit rock bottom and there seemed to be no way out; suicide seemed to be the only solution. I'd had enough of life and just wanted to escape from all the problems I was faced with.

The major worry on my mind was the fact that my career as a footballer was in ruins. I'd won the League title with Leeds United and should have been looking forward to a few more years in the game, but a bad injury forced me to quit playing and I hadn't come to terms with the fact that my career was over. I just didn't know what I was going to do next because all I knew was football. Added to that, financial problems had forced me and my wife Charmaine to put our house up for sale and there was no sign of a buyer.

When everything started going wrong, there was nobody there to help me.

Mel STERLAND

I'd come to a crossroads in my life and I simply just didn't know which way to turn. I felt as though I'd been cast out into the wilderness and just told to get on with my life. There was no-one I could turn to. People like agents, for example, only want to know you when the going is good. When you're no good to them anymore, they just drop you like a ton of bricks.

To escape from all the misery, I turned to drink and got drunk on a regular basis. I would then drive while still under the influence of alcohol and do all sorts of things I shouldn't have been doing. The alcohol only made things worse of course because it makes you depressed if you have too much of it.

After another heavy drinking session, I just got to the point where I thought, "Right, I've had enough, I'm going to end it all." Thoughts of suicide had been on my mind a couple of months before, but I'd done nothing about it. This time it was different; I wanted to end my life and the only question was how I'd actually go about doing it. I'd thought about getting hold of some tablets and taking an overdose before deciding to connect a hosepipe to the exhaust pipe on my car.

I hadn't told anybody just how depressed I felt, so nobody suspected a thing. When you're planning to do something as extreme as topping yourself, it's something you keep to yourself. I believe that if you're going to commit suicide, you just do it. Perhaps if I had talked my problems through with someone who was prepared to listen, things would have been different and I wouldn't have got to the stage where I wanted to end my life.

I still get emotional when I think back to the day when I was ready to end it all; I can remember it as if it was yesterday. It was a Monday and I still felt hung-over from the night before. We had a large garden, so I used to water it with a hosepipe which I retrieved from my garage. I then put the hosepipe into the boot of my car, a blue Mercedes, and drove out into the Derbyshire countryside. I needed a remote spot, a place where I wouldn't be disturbed, to enable me to carry out my plan. We lived at the north-east tip of Derbyshire, in a town called Dronfield, so there were plenty of open spaces within easy reach.

My head was in a spin, so I wasn't even sure where I was going when I set off. I eventually decided to head for the picturesque village of Hathersage, about 10 miles away. I knew the area well because one of my brothers lived there. After pulling up on a side road, I immediately stepped out of my car and set everything up. I took the hosepipe out of the boot, cut it down and clipped it on to the exhaust. I then opened the rear window on the driver's side and put the hosepipe through it. After getting back into the driver's seat and closing the door, I wound up the rear door window to trap the hosepipe.

I just sat there for a few minutes, thinking about my family and crying my eyes out. Then after looking at the beautiful countryside scene in front of me for one last time, I said to myself, "Here goes, let's do it". I turned the key in the ignition and the engine started up. Moments later, before the fumes had a chance to take effect, I heard a voice in my head, which I'm sure was my mum, saying, "Oi, you daft bastard, you've got a lovely wife and two great kids, what are you doing?" Those words made me snap out of it. I turned the engine off and thought, "What ARE you doing, you silly twat? There's more to life than football".

Mel STERLAND

I'm not a spiritual person; I don't even believe in God because my mum was taken from us when I was still a teenager and he's also taken my brother George and my sister Avril before their time. But I believe my mum was looking out for me when I came close to ending it all that day. Her words stopped me from doing something stupid.

I was in my car for about an hour, thinking how stupid I'd been to even consider killing myself. After finally managing to compose myself, I made the 20 minute journey home. Once I got home, I poured myself a stiff drink to calm my nerves. Later, when I came into contact with family and friends, I acted as though nothing had happened.

I think if I had gone through with it, people would probably have said, "Oh, he's committed suicide, he's a coward, the gutless bastard." But I disagree with that way of thinking because I believe it takes guts to commit suicide. Whether it's putting a rope round your neck, taking an overdose or whatever, it's not an easy thing to do at all.

My missus knew of course that I was depressed about being forced to quit playing, but she didn't know I'd seriously contemplated suicide until about two months after that fateful day. I told her sister, Sarah, that I'd wanted to end it all. She then told Charmaine, who brought the subject up one day. I was crying as I told Charmaine exactly what had happened. I admitted that I'd got so down that I intended to end it all and explained that I went as far as fixing a hosepipe to the exhaust and starting the ignition before coming to my senses. She could hardly take in what I was saying and started crying. Then there was a mixture of upset and anger as she laid into me. "You fucking selfish bastard," she shouted, unable to contain her emotions. "How could you even think about doing that? There's me, Chantelle and Nathan to think about for a start and I'd have to pick the pieces up."

There were some more dark days to follow as I struggled to come to terms with the end of my football career. Thankfully, however, I never seriously thought about committing suicide again.

CHAPTER TWO

To The Manor Born

When my mum was pregnant with me and my twin brother Glyn, she was on her own when she went into labour. She needed some money for the bus fare to take her to hospital and the only cash she could find were the coins on top of the pools coupon, which had been left on the mantelpiece, ready to be handed over to the collector who came to the door.

After me and Glyn were born on 1 October 1961, my dad checked the pools coupon, which had been left on the mantelpiece and worked out that it would have been a big win. I don't know how much they would have won, but instead of landing a big windfall, they ended up with two babies. I find it ironic that I was involved in a missed opportunity to win at gambling before I was even born!

Boozing, Betting & Brawling

Me and Glyn were the last additions to a family of nine kids raised by my mum, Lillian and dad, George. Because they were elderly parents, everybody thought my dad was my granddad. Already on the scene were my brothers George, Terry, John and Malcolm and my sisters Sharon, Sheila and Avril. There's a big gap in ages because I'm 46 and my eldest brother is 63. George and Avril are sadly no longer with us. George, who had diabetes, died a few years ago in his early fifties and Avril was only 39 when she died of cancer.

When we were young kids, my mum would ask me and Glyn to nick a fag from our George's bedroom. Glyn wouldn't go up because he was scared of George, so I used to cop for it. George was a big lad, about 6ft 5ins tall, and he could be ruthless. He used to throw a shoe at me if he caught me creeping into his room.

We've got gypsy blood in the family, on my mum's side. My parents knew a lot of travellers, or "didicois" as we used to call them. They came regularly to our house in these big, old caravans, carrying a load of scrap. My mum always made them welcome and she cooked them a turkey at Christmas. Ironically, when I became a footballer, opposition fans used to chant "Gypo" and "Where's your caravan?" at me because of my long hair.

My mum and dad, who have both passed away, worked hard to support the family. My mum was a polisher at Viners cutlery manufacturers in Sheffield and she later worked in a school kitchen. I lost my mum when I was 18, which was a bit cruel really. My dad was a steel erector who worked away a lot and I was 22 or 23 when he died. My parents were a great couple and it was sad to see them pass away when they did.

We had a hard upbringing on the tough Manor estate in Sheffield. You had to look after yourself and if you weren't street-wise, you'd get punished. Mum and Dad always told me to be careful and they'd sometimes warn me about certain people. They'd say, "Don't knock about with him because he's a bad 'un."

We lived in a little three-bedroom semi-detached house with an outside toilet. The house has been knocked down, but I often drive past the site where it stood and think, "We had a rough upbringing, but it was great to live there." It wasn't a comfortable existence, by any stretch of the imagination, but we made do. We had to scrimp and scrape for everything and we had to be content with a holiday in Chapel St Leonards every year. We went to the same place, without fail. We stayed in a caravan at first and then we got posh and moved up to a chalet!

Mum used to buy about seven loaves of bread a day to feed us all. You look back and think, "Bloody hell, how did we manage?" But we did because we had to. With so many of us in the family, it was a case of first up, best dressed. As the youngest in the family, me and Glyn got the "pass-downs" – clothes that had been worn by our elder brothers.

When I was very young, one of my sisters, Sheila, spent all her wages to win a goldfish for me and our Glyn at the fairground. She had a number of goes at a particular game before finally succeeding and winning the goldfish which she gave to me when she got home. A couple of hours later, all the family sat

Boozing, Betting & Brawling

down to eat in the kitchen, apart from me because I was preoccupied with my new goldfish. After a while, Sheila sensed that I was up to something. "He's quiet," she said to the rest of the family before going outside to find out what I was doing. She was horrified to find that I'd chopped the goldfish up into little pieces. "What have you done that for?" she shouted. "It wouldn't walk," I told her. I'd taken the fish out of the small plastic bag filled with water it was happily swimming in and expected it to walk on the ground. When it just flapped about, I decided to chop it up for some reason. Sheila went crazy because she'd spent all her money winning a goldfish which I then promptly butchered!

I have to hold my hand up to another act of cruelty towards an animal when I was a kid. We had a budgie and when I put my finger through the bars of its cage one day, it pecked me. "You bastard," I screamed as I jumped back, clutching the finger that had been pecked. "Right, I'll show you," I thought as I decided to exact my revenge on the budgie. I went and found our cat, picked it up, went back to the cage and put it in with the budgie. Fortunately for the budgie, one of my sisters came into the room and grabbed the cat before it had a chance to attack.

I went to Pitworth School, which was only round the corner from where we lived. I still sucked on a dummy when I started school and the other kids used to give me a lot of stick over that. My mum and dad used to go bonkers when I insisted on taking the dummy to school.

At the perimeter of the school playground there were some iron railings and kids used to squeeze through them. After seeing some lads go through the railings, I decided to follow them. There was a wall below the railings which I put my feet on before trying to clamber my way through, but my head was too big and I got stuck! I couldn't move and someone called the emergency services, telling them about my predicament. A chair was brought out for me to stand on and I just had to wait there while the fire engine came. It was more embarrassing than anything else because there were kids and parents all laughing at me. I was probably stuck there for about 20-25 minutes but it seemed like two or three hours. When the firemen arrived they bent the railings at either side of my head to free me. That incident resulted in me getting my name in the newspaper years before I made headlines as a footballer. A short piece appeared in the *Sheffield Star*, with a headline saying something along the lines of "Schoolboy Traps Head in Railings".

I started knocking a ball about with Glyn when we were seven. I can remember one Christmas, Mum and Dad went out and bought us some white boots which must have cost a fortune. The boots were out of a catalogue and they paid a small amount every week.

When Dad saw me and Glyn kicking a ball about at the age of 10 or 11 – we might have been even younger – he said that one or both of us would make it as professionals. In fact, he was going to have a bet on me playing for England when I was a kid and went as far as writing out a betting slip, but he didn't get round to putting it on.

When I wasn't getting my head stuck between railings, I used to kick a ball about in the schoolyard and dream about being a professional footballer. I'd think about what it must be like to run out on the pitch at Hillsborough and play for Sheffield Wednesday.

It was one of my brothers, our Terry, who was instrumental in me becoming a Sheffield Wednesday supporter. Terry was a mad keen Wednesday fan who followed them home and away. One day when he was preparing to watch Wednesday, he turned to me and said, "Do you want to go to the game?" I didn't need asking twice so we went to Hillsborough and stood on the Kop, but I can't remember who we played that day. Whenever I went to matches, I'd watch the players and think, "One day that might be me." I used to love Tommy Craig, who was a Scottish midfielder. When I looked at him, I just thought what a great professional he was. He was a fantastic player and a good athlete with a great left foot. I saw him years later at a dinner at Sheffield Wednesday and asked him for his autograph. "Tommy, can you sign this because you were my hero," I said. He started laughing and said, "Fuck off!" because he knew where I'd been and what I'd done in my career. I said, "No, honestly" and he signed a card.

My brother-in-law, our Brian, worked on the turnstiles at Sheffield United, so he sometimes used to take me to games at Bramall Lane where I'd help him collect the money. We were on the turnstiles and we'd sometimes let fans jump over the turnstile if they paid about 50p. That meant that the turnstile didn't click, so it didn't register just how many fans had passed through and we could pocket the cash.

It was always Sheffield Wednesday for me, but our Glyn decided to support

Mel STERLAND

Sheffield United. I think he was just being an awkward bleeder! It was pretty much a 50/50 split at school between fans of Sheffield Wednesday and Sheffield United. I can't remember there being many kids who supported any other clubs. Wednesday were struggling when I was growing up, but they were still getting big crowds. I can remember the game at home to Southend on the last day of the 1973/74 season, which they had to win to avoid going down to the old Third Division. They managed to do so, with Ken Knighton scoring the winner just five minutes from time. There were no such last day heroics the following season when, with five games still to play, Wednesday were relegated to the Third Division for the first time in the history of the club.

As a young kid on the Manor, we used to pinch bottles from a pub and take them to the local shop so we could get the deposit money. You used to get a penny or something. We also used to go "egging" which basically involved climbing trees and collecting birds' eggs. We were egging once when my cousin, a lad called Charles Christian, was attacked by a bird when he reached over to the nest for the eggs. He fell out of the tree and had a fit when he landed on the ground. He was screaming and it was obvious he was in a lot of pain, so we called for an ambulance and left him to wait for it at the side of the road. It turned out that he'd broken his leg in the fall.

We also used to play "knock and run". You'd knock on someone's door and then run off before they answered it. We loved it if someone came out of the house and chased you. There was a guy called Mr Hackett who followed me home once and accused me of nicking his doorbell, of all things. All I'd done

Boozing, Betting & Brawling

was knock on his door, but he saw my mum and told her I'd taken his doorbell. My dad was strict and when he found out that Mr Hackett had been round, he gave me a good hiding.

It was natural for those from families who hadn't got much money to make things to play with, using whatever was freely available. Kids from families who had a bit of money would have had go-karts bought for them, but we'd got nowt of course so we made what we called trolleys. We'd take an old pram and put big wheels at the back, small wheels at the front and then attach string to a make-shift axle to steer it.

When I was about 13, I was with our Glyn one day and we were messing about with a trolley we'd just made, using some nails we'd managed to scrounge. We were with mates who also had trolleys and we were racing each other on the roads and pavements near our house. Then my brother Malcolm came along and he wanted to have a go on our trolley. When we wouldn't let him, he jumped on the trolley and broke it in half. I was fuming because I wanted to race with it and there weren't any nails left to repair it. The closest thing to hand was a hammer, which we'd used when we were making the trolley, so I picked that up and chased after Malcolm. He ran off up the road with me in hot pursuit, raising the hammer above my head and shouting angrily, "I'll fucking put this in your head." A police car then appeared and pulled over just in front of me, so I stopped running. The police officers in the car obviously wanted to know why I was chasing after someone with a hammer in my hand, threatening to use it. "What are you doing?" he asked after getting out of the car.

Mel STERLAND

"I'm going to get him" I replied.

"What do you mean, you're going to get him?"

"He's my brother and he's jumped on my trolley and broken it. I can't repair it because I've got no fucking nails left."

After telling me to stop swearing, he asked where I lived and then told me to get in the car. We made the short trip to our house and the policeman had a word with my parents, telling them what I had been caught doing. That resulted in me getting a clip round the head from my dad. Looking back, it was a good job that I was caught because I'd have definitely hit Malcolm with the hammer. I was so mad because we hadn't got any money to buy some more nails, so that was us done.

I was playing as much football as I could, having got into a team based at the Three Feathers pub, which wasn't far from where I lived, at the age of nine or 10. The manager of the Three Feathers team was Mr Martin – who we called "Doc" Martin – and he was a great guy. I was playing for the Under-12s as a centre-forward and I used to score goals for fun.

One particular Sunday, a couple of Sheffield Wednesday scouts, Charlie Wain and Eric Gyte, came to watch us. They approached me at the end of the game and said, "Do you fancy coming down to Sheffield Wednesday?" I thought they were taking the piss, to be honest, because they didn't even look like scouts. They were two big guys who looked more like policemen.

I went home and excitedly told my mum and dad about the invitation to go to Wednesday. They were pleased for me and encouraged me to go for it. I'd moved a step closer to realising my dream of playing for Wednesday.

CHAPTER THREE

The Bog Brush Man

I went to Wednesday's training ground on a Tuesday to train under a bloke called Robin Wray. I found it was very hard because I was only a young lad and I wasn't used to it. I can remember being sick after finishing training. I went back again for training two days later and then played for the Three Feathers on the Sunday.

I never thought much about it until I received a letter from Sheffield Wednesday, telling me I'd been selected to train at the club on Tuesdays and Thursdays, with the aim of hopefully playing for Wednesday's nursery side, Middlewood Rovers.

It wasn't long before I did start playing for Middlewood Rovers which was great because they were the top Sunday League side. I was with Charlie

Boozing, Betting & Brawling

Williamson who I of course knew from school. Charlie Wain and Eric Gyte used to come and watch both of us playing for the school team. There was a teacher called Mr Bainbridge who ran the school team. He was a fantastic guy and he did well with the team, taking us to the semi-finals of a competition. Me and Charlie were among three players in that side who turned pro, the other being Carl Shutt. A couple of other lads who did well in that side were Trevor Jones and Steve Brown. Years after leaving school, when I was established in the Wednesday first-team, I saw Mr Bainbridge one day at Hillsborough, queuing up for tickets. I had a chat with him and still called him "Sir" because it sticks. It's like when I see Howard Wilkinson now, I still call him "Gaffer".

I finally got in the Sheffield Boys side at Under-14 level, a couple of years after going with Charlie Williamson for an unsuccessful trial. When we didn't get in the first time, we thought it was probably down to the fact that we were off the Manor because Sheffield Boys at that time was made up of lads from families who'd got money.

Things went well from there and I was selected for Wednesday's Northern Intermediate side. I would say that's the hardest league to play in as a kid. It's all different now, there's no Northern Intermediate League because clubs have Academies. But you can speak to any footballer from my era and they'll tell you that the Northern Intermediate was the hardest league to play in.

I signed schoolboy forms for Wednesday at the age of 15. Once you had signed blue forms, you couldn't go anywhere else, but that didn't bother me because all I wanted to do was to play for Wednesday. I had offers from elsewhere before I signed for Wednesday. I can remember being sat in our house with Charlie Wain and Eric Gyte and the phone was ringing with Sunderland, Birmingham, Rotherham and Lincoln all wanting to sign me. Wednesday were desperate to avoid losing me to another club. I'd got Charlie and Eric there and Wednesday's youth coach, Ken Knighton, was on the phone saying, "Come and sign for Sheffield Wednesday, you'll love it at Hillsborough." My mum and dad left it up to me to decide. "It's up to you," they said, "do what you want to do." Choosing a club to sign for is a big decision at such a young age, but there was never really ever any doubt over who I was going to join. I wanted to sign for Wednesday and apart from anything else, I didn't want to live away from home. I signed the schoolboy forms there and then.

Our Glyn was a very good footballer and quite a few clubs were watching him as well. Sunderland and Birmingham both wanted to sign him on schoolboy forms but he wasn't bothered. He wasn't disciplined and as he got older, all he wanted to do was go out with women and drink. Glyn loved it when I made it as a player and used to come to matches, but he used to tell all his mates he was a better footballer than me. I just took it in my stride, but we had a fall-out once when he said he was better than me, insisting that it was him who should have made it. "Well I was fucking better than you," he said. "Well why didn't you do it then?" I said. "You just wanted to fucking go out drinking and shagging birds." There was no lasting bitterness though. I think he sometimes regrets not giving it a go, but he was proud of what I achieved in the game and we're so close now it's untrue. He works as a butcher in South Anston.

Boozing, Betting & Brawling

Len Ashurst was the manager when I first joined Wednesday. He had big, bushy eyebrows and used to scare me to death! I didn't have much to do with him because in those days they didn't bother about the kids. Len had more important things to do than look at us because he'd got the first-team to worry about. He was replaced as manager by Jack Charlton early in the 1977/78 season.

When I was 16, before I signed as an apprentice with Wednesday, I worked at Sutherland's factory in Sheffield. I couldn't sign for Wednesday until a certain date so my sister Avril, who worked at Sutherland's, got me a job there. A mate of mine from school called Paul Galley also got a job there and we had to unload a thousand frozen lambs. That was proper work, getting up at four in the morning and finishing about 12 hours later. I was only a skinny thing back then and the lambs were heavy. I couldn't wait to finish that job and become a footballer.

When I became an apprentice at Hillsborough, we had all sorts of jobs to do around the ground. We had to clean the toilets, wash the showers and clean all the boots. Everyone had certain jobs to do. The coaches were really keen and made sure you did your job right. If you didn't do it right, you got your arse kicked. I can remember one Friday when we were running late and we finally got off at about 4.45pm. Maurice Setters was the assistant manager and he ordered us all to report back at around 6pm because someone hadn't cleaned one of the window ledges. Maurice had run his finger along the window ledge and found it was thick with dust. One of the lads, Craig Howard, had to come

Mel STERLAND

all the way back from Worksop.

We were all given certain players' boots to look after and it was my job to look after the ones belonging to Rodger Wylde, Chris Turner, Jeff Johnson and Mick Pickering. They were older professionals and you had to respect them, otherwise you'd get a clip round the ear-hole. You couldn't answer them back. If their boots were dirty, they'd kick your arse. If the cleaning wasn't done to their satisfaction, they'd give you a bollocking. Wylde and Turner were horrible bastards! At Christmas time they'd never give you any tips. As a young kid, you used to look forward to getting a Christmas present off your players, but not off Rodger or Chris – they didn't give you a penny. Johnson wasn't any better because he just used to ignore you. All three of them were great guys – just tight bleeders! But Pickering was brilliant – he was top drawer. Everyone wanted to be given his boots to clean because he looked after the apprentices. He might only give you a fiver or a tenner, but as a young kid on peanuts, even that was fantastic. Another of the older pros, Ian Porterfield, who's sadly no longer with us, was a diamond. He used to stay at the end of training and train with us.

As well as making sure the boots were clean, the stripes on the boots had to be white because of the sponsorship. It had to be done right and if it wasn't, you'd get a bollocking. We also had to do maintenance work on the stadium, so in pre-season we'd clean the stand and paint it. I think the discipline we had was fantastic. Today's youngsters who're just starting out in the game miss out on that because I think they now employ people to clean the boots. That's a shame, in my opinion, because it's all about learning your trade. If you go into a factory, for example, you start at the bottom of the ladder and work your way up. Perhaps youngsters coming into the game now have it too easy.

As apprentices, we were also in charge of looking after the footballs and the various other bits of equipment in training. The balls had to be blown up properly and the bibs had to be put out, ready for the players to use. I remember one occasion when I went up to the training ground with some of the other apprentices, ahead of a first-team training session. Big-hitters like Jeff Johnson, Rodger Wylde and Brian Hornsby turned up for training with the rest of the senior pros and they did some shooting practice before having a five-a-side game. I was put in charge of the balls that day and that meant that I had to make sure none of them were lost during the session.

Jack Charlton was stood to one side of the penalty area and he was playing short passes to players who had to run up and strike the ball at goal. When it came to Johnson's turn, he ran up and struck the ball with a lot of power but no accuracy. His shot was so off-target that the ball cleared the fence at the perimeter of the training ground, ending up in some waste ground at the other side of the fence. Nobody used to like going into that area because it was overgrown, full of nettles and brambles, but I knew that I'd have to go and retrieve the ball.

"Mel, you're in charge of that ball," Jack shouted to remind me as I headed for the fence. "Make sure you fucking get it because if you don't there'll be thirty quid coming out of your wages." I didn't even get thirty quid, so I don't know where he got that figure from! I think I was on £26-a-week at the time so the thought of losing that sort of money made me panic like mad. I quickly got over the fence and saw that the ball had gone into the River Don, which was in the middle of the waste ground. I got hold of a large stick to try and force the ball to the side of the river and I was messing about for ages because the ball was bobbing about on the water and kept getting stuck on some large stones jutting out above the surface. When I managed to free the ball, it kept drifting downstream and of course I had to follow it. It kept going and going until it was level with the players' entrance at Hillsborough – which is some distance from the training ground – and I waded into the water and got it. I jogged back to the training ground with the ball under my arm and Jack was laughing his head off when he saw me. "Oh, you were panicking about having to fucking pay for it, weren't you?!" he said. He might have been laughing but I think he would have made me pay for the ball if I hadn't brought it back.

We used to have loads of scraps and get into mischief when we were apprentices. The head groundsman at Hillsborough was called Dave Barber, who was a great guy. He had a scooter and one of the other apprentices, a lad called Craig Howard, said he could ride it. One day Craig started up Dave's scooter and told me to get on the back, so I did and we went round the back of the North Stand. Everything was okay until Craig did a wheelie and hit a wall, throwing us both off. The scooter was smashed up and it soon became obvious that it was a write-off. Dave, who loved his scooter, went crying to Jack Charlton, telling him that me and Craig had smashed it up, which of course we

Boozing, Betting & Brawling

had done. Jack obviously wasn't happy about that and gave us both a bollocking. So we roped everyone else in and there were about six or seven who got the blame for it. I think we all got about two or three quid a week taken out of our wages for a while because of that.

Doc Purcell, who was the club doctor, was a really eccentric character. He was like someone out of the film, *One Flew Over The Cuckoo's Nest* with his wild hair and glasses. He often used to come in with bits of tissue stuck to his face, where he'd cut himself shaving. I saw him with two ties round his neck one day. "Doc, what are you doing with two ties on?" I asked. "Two ties?" he replied, totally oblivious to the fact that he'd got one tie hanging down from his collar as normal and the other slung over his shoulder. His wife used to nag him so much that he didn't know what he was doing half the time. He'd probably put the first tie on and then, because she was going on and on at him, put another one on without thinking. A few young players used to lodge at Doc Purcell's house so we'd often go there for something to eat after training. He had an Old English Sheepdog which left a turd in the middle of the surgery one day when we were there.

There was a big Welsh lad, known as "Taffy" who suffered a rather unfortunate injury which required stitches when we were messing about in the communal bath one day. When Taffy tried to jump out of the bath, he slipped and caught himself on a broken tile. You could see blood and we were all laughing because we just thought that he'd cut his leg. It turned out that he'd actually cut his bollocks and had to go and see the physio to have some stitches put in. After passing Taffy in the corridor, Jack Charlton came into the dressing room, laughing and shouting, "He's cut his ballacks open." Everybody just burst out laughing because it was funny to hear the manager saying something like that.

There was a sort of initiation ceremony for apprentices at Hillsborough, known as a "blacking". I suppose it's like when someone gets a job at a steelworks or wherever and the boss tells them to go for a long stand or a right-handed screwdriver. People fall for it because they don't know what it's all about.

The apprentices used to use the away dressing room at Hillsborough and that was where the punishment started. If you were picked out for a blacking, you'd be set upon by the others. You were held down while the others punched and kicked you. It was no good just accepting your punishment and telling them to get on with it. You had to put a fight up because if you didn't, you'd have it done to you again a month or two later, so you had to smack a few. But no matter how much you tried to defend yourself, you knew that you'd end up having all sorts of unpleasant things done to you because you were heavily out-numbered.

Firstly, after being stripped bollock-naked, Vaseline and boot polish would be put on your bollocks. Deep Heat, which is used to relieve muscular aches and pains, was also put on your bollocks and your knob, causing a real stinging sensation. Vaseline would be rubbed in your hair, up your arse and in your ears. When it came to my turn to dish out the punishment, I was the "bog brush man". I'd get a really hard toilet brush, shove it into their bollocks – which were covered in Vaseline and boot polish by this time – and twirl it round. They'd be screaming in agony, which was great because I'd had it done to me by Craig Howard. I can remember that as if it was yesterday.

After all that, you'd be tied to the treatment bench, carried out onto the pitch and left in the centre-circle. You were left there, stretched out, until you managed to wriggle free. Nobody could help you because if they did, they'd have the same done to them. There were some who were left there for six or seven hours.

David Grant recalls me and Gordon Simmonite being the ring-leaders during his blacking. He says that we stripped him off and then used some old socks to tie him to the treatment table before taking him out on to the Kop, where we left him in the freezing cold. We got all the women working at the club, from those working in the washer room to the office staff, to go and take a look at "Granty" freezing his nuts off! None of them were allowed to free him and he spent two hours tied up there.

Another lad was tied to the fencing at the top of the Kop. It was before there was a roof on the Kop, so people driving past the ground on Penistone Road could see this shivering, bollock-naked lad, covered in boot polish and Vaseline.

An alternative punishment was to cover the apprentice in Vaseline and boot polish before putting them in a skip used to store dirty kit. We'd then take the skip into the shower area and piss on him while he tried to cover up his head. Then after having warm piss on him, he'd be put under a cold shower.

Taffy had permed hair and we made a right mess of that with all the grease and boot polish. He was left tied-up in the skip outside the players' entrance and when an old woman lifted up the lid, he jumped up, thinking it was the other apprentices, nearly giving her a heart attack. I think she reported the incident to Jack Charlton, telling him that one of the players had been hiding in the skip with nothing on.

The older pros used to love it when someone had a blacking. They'd be asking you who was going to get done next. Then when a blacking was taking place, they used to watch. It was horrible when it was your turn, but it was a great laugh and nobody complained about it when I was there. You just had to take it on the chin.

On another occasion when I had to go to see someone in the club shop, I felt a burning sensation on my wedding tackle. My balls and knob felt like they were on fire. The woman I had gone to see gave me an odd look because I was playing with my balls, trying to sort it out. When I went back to the changing room, I saw that my balls and knob-end were red-raw. I didn't know what had caused it until Brian Hornsby owned up to putting some Algipan (a rub used to provide temporary warming relief from muscular pain) in my pants!

When I was an apprentice, Jack Charlton used to take us out into the woods to do some beating while he was shooting. We had to make bird noises and beat the undergrowth so that pheasants would fly up for him and his friends to shoot. He had all the apprentices doing that so we didn't know whether we were footballers or farmers! When the shoot was over, Jack would treat us to fish and chips. Jack also had us cleaning his car but we didn't mind doing that because there was always loads of spare change under the seats which

Boozing, Betting & Brawling

we used to pocket.

When you were an apprentice, the club paid your board, so at least that was taken care of. You were handed the money in an envelope to hand over to your parents, or whoever you were lodging with, and they had to sign a receipt to say they'd received it.

I was still an apprentice when I broke into the first-team at the age of 17. Jack Charlton decided to name me as a substitute for the game at home to Blackpool on 17 May 1979 and I came on as a 78th minute replacement for Brian Hornsby on the right-hand side of midfield. It was a freezing cold night. Jack just told me to go out there and enjoy it, but I was frightened to death. The crowd was only just over 7,000 but it seemed like 70,000 to me. We won 2-0 with goals from Ian Porterfield and Gordon Owen.

The final game of the season, at home to Hull City, was just two days later and I wondered whether I'd feature in that. When we had a practice match in training, I was included in the first-team against the reserves. I thought to myself, "Bloody hell, I must be playing on Saturday." Jack never said anything to me though and you never knew with him because he used to change his mind so many times. But sure enough, when the team-sheet went up on the Friday, my name was on it, which was a great feeling.

My brother Glyn forecast that I'd score and my dad put some money on me scoring.

Thankfully, I managed to win some money for him. I got the ball, knocked it wide to Gordon Owen who pulled it back to me on the edge of the box and

Mel STERLAND

I whacked it into the net with my right foot. After the goal went in, I saw my mum and dad jumping up and getting really excited. They were delighted for me and were clearly very proud.

Kevin Taylor was another youngster in the side and assistant manager Maurice Setters praised us both after the game. In the *Sheffield Morning Telegraph*, Jim Ferguson wrote, "Sterland justified his sudden promotion to the first-team with an equaliser after 20 minutes in his first full league match."

Despite the fact that I'd played in a couple of league games, I was not even a professional footballer, but I was about to become one.

CHAPTER FOUR

"Sign That Or Fucking Get Out"

I signed as a professional when I was 17. They didn't usually sign you as a pro until you turned 18, but they brought the date forward in my case because of the fact that I was in the first-team. I went home to tell my mum and dad that I'd got to go in and see Jack Charlton because they wanted me to sign as a professional. Obviously, I didn't have an agent then, so I asked my dad how much I should ask for. "Well, ask for two hundred and fifty quid," he said.

"Bloody hell Dad, that's a lot of money you know," I replied.

"Well, you're in the first-team – you've got to go in high and let him knock you down," he advised.

Mel STERLAND

So I went to Jack's office, absolutely frightened to death; I was shitting myself! I knocked on the door and Big Jack called me in. When I opened the door, he was sat there, wearing a flat cap, reading a newspaper and smoking a fag. He told me to sit down before asking, "What do you want?" I was frightened to death with sweat pouring down my face and thinking, "Right, I've got to hit him with this now." Trembling, I spluttered, "What about two hundred and fifty quid?" Well, he nearly choked on his fag; his head dropped down and his cap fell onto the floor. There was no negotiating, he just said, "Look son, sign that or fucking get out." I just wanted to get out of the room as quickly as possible, so I signed the contract he put in front of me straight away, not really taking in the details. I later discovered that the contract was for fifty quid a week, with sixty quid appearance money. When I went back home and saw my father, I said, "Thanks a lot Dad, for that."

As a young professional, I was able to afford a car. The first car I bought was an old Ford Escort Mk I. It cost me three hundred and fifty quid and I got ripped off good style over that because the gearbox was filled with sawdust! I was driving to the training ground one day with Charlie Williamson in the passenger seat and the gearstick came off in my hand! Charlie was laughing his bollocks off because he had a better car than me. He played against Sheffield United in the "Boxing Day Massacre" and with his win bonus and crowd bonus from that game, he bought a Hillman Imp.

My next car was a Vauxhall Chevette and I got ripped off with that as well. I bought it on finance for about a grand and it was a bag of crap. The exhaust

Boozing, Betting & Brawling

was knackered and people could hear me arriving down the road because of all the banging and popping. I got a sponsored car with my name written all over it when I became a first-team regular. It was a beautiful white VW Golf from a dealership in Sheffield called Gilders. I drove into the centre of Sheffield one night, parked up and went into a nightclub. When it was time to go home, I saw that some bastard had puked up all over my windscreen. It must have been a Sheffield United fan!

With the Chevette surplus to requirements when I took delivery of the sponsored Golf, I gave it to my brother Glyn. I told him that he'd have to take over the finance payments, which worked out at around twenty quid a month. "Yeah, no problem, I'll do that," he said. A few months later, there was a knock on the door one day and when I answered it, the guy standing there said, "Are you Mr Sterland?" When I told him I was, he explained that he was a bailiff acting on behalf of the finance company I'd taken the finance out with for the car. He said that he'd come to recover the car because I hadn't paid the finance. He wanted to know where the car was because he had a car transporter with him. I told him that I no longer had the car, but I still had to pay about a hundred quid to clear the debt. I later found out that Glyn had sold the car for about three or four hundred quid, kept the money and not paid the finance.

I failed to get into the starting line-up during the 1979/80 season and had to settle for three substitute appearances. We went into the last game of the season, away at Exeter, competing with Chesterfield for the last promotion spot. I was the 13th man that day, so I was sat on the bench with the backroom staff.

Mel STERLAND

Before kick-off, when Jack Charlton joined us, he saw some felt hanging over one end of the bench, which he assumed was still part of it. He went to sit down and because there was nothing underneath the felt, he fell backwards, shouting, "Fucking hell" as he collapsed onto the ground at the back of the dug-out. Nobody dared laugh, of course, even though it was so funny to watch.

Even though we lost 1-0, with Mark Smith missing a penalty, we still won promotion that day because Chesterfield went down to a defeat at Millwall. Going up to the Second Division obviously meant a step-up in quality.

I started playing more the following season but I didn't enjoy it because I didn't know where to run and I wasn't sure when I wanted the ball. I received so much stick from the fans and it was just a nightmare. When the fans saw my name on the team-sheet in midfield, I think they used to go, "Oh fucking hell, he's playing again, that Sterland!" It was horrible because it wasn't working out. I started as a forward scoring goals for the Northern Intermediate side, but then I seemed to be going backwards. I went from being a forward to a midfield player and as a midfielder it was very hard.

I thought I was going to get released at the end of the season and I seriously wanted to pack in playing. But it was a matter of getting my head down, working hard and doing extra training. I was lucky because there were some good pros there who helped me. Mick Pickering was great, a really good pro. He used to sit you down and talk to you, telling you where you were going wrong.

Jack Charlton obviously thought I was worth persevering with, despite the fact that I was hardly pulling up any trees in midfield. After we won 1-0 at home to

Boozing, Betting & Brawling

Watford in November 1980, Jack praised my performance. "Mel Sterland did well and is an honest lad who will get better as he gets older," he told the Press after the game.

Our trainer was an ex-Marine called Tony Toms, who was a very hard man. He was a great guy, but he used to frighten us to death. When you went down in a game, you'd get up as quickly as possible when he came on to treat you because you knew what was going to happen. His idea of treatment was to shower you in cold water by chucking the "magic sponge" at you and then shout, "Get up you soft bastard!"

When you reported for training, "Tomsy" would come over to you to ask what time it was. Then when you glanced at your watch, he'd grab your wrist, bend it back and pick you up off the floor. You'd be screaming like a baby, but he knew how far to go without injuring you.

I remember going in for treatment once on a Sunday when I went through the changing room and found Tomsy in the big communal bath with a couple of birds. I couldn't believe it. Obviously he didn't think anybody would be in that day. "Fucking get out," he shouted at me. I wasn't going to argue with him so I got out of the way sharpish and left them to it.

In February 1981, Tomsy organised for us to go down to the Commando Training Centre in Lymstone, near Exeter. I think Tomsy wanted to put us through our paces and toughen us up. We arrived at the centre in our coach and saw all these young Marines running around. We all gathered round and the guy in charge told us what we'd be doing. The Sergeant Major crucified one young

Mel STERLAND

Marine who was struggling to complete the assault course. We felt sorry for this young lad because he was getting so much stick. "If you don't fucking do it, you'll be going round the run again," shouted the Sergeant Major. That would have meant him doing something like a five-mile run and the lad was so demoralised he started crying.

The following day, it was our turn to go out on the course, which was a real experience. It was raining and we had to go through freezing cold water, dipping down into a tunnel underneath the water. When you emerged at the other side of the tunnel, they pulled you out of the water by your hair. It was scary. Our Yugoslavian midfielder, Ante Mirocevic, took one look at the water and refused to do it. "No, not me," he said, shaking his head, "no fucking way." A few other players also decided against doing it but I wanted to have a go. Once that was out of the way, you had to do all sorts of things like climb ropes and swing down.

While we were at the training centre, we were also taken to a swimming pool and told to get in the water while dressed in commando trousers, with a helmet on and wearing shoes. To make it even harder, we also had to carry a pack and a rifle. We were told to tread water for a couple of minutes, swim a length, tread water again, then take your rifle off, which was slung over your shoulder on a strap, and then remove your clothes. It was really difficult but I managed to do it. I looked over and saw Bob Bolder, who was sinking. He couldn't get his rifle over his head and his arm was locked so Tomsy had to jump into the water and pull him out.

Boozing, Betting & Brawling

Tomsy pointed out a balcony at the centre which was known as the "Tony Toms Balcony" from his time there. He told us that they'd gone out for a few beers one night and when they returned to the centre, he did a hand-stand on the balcony, which was high up. Tomsy got involved in personal security work after leaving football and ended up doing some work as a minder for Madonna.

Our time at Lymstone was something different to playing football and it brought all the players together. I couldn't imagine them doing that sort of thing now. I don't think the big-name players in the Premiership, especially the foreigners, would fancy having a go at something like that.

My big break came when our right-back, Ray Blackhall, was injured in the build-up to the game at Luton in September 1981 and Jack Charlton was debating over who would take his place. Chief scout John Harris said, "Put Mel at right-back." Jack obviously wasn't impressed with the idea because he was effing and blinding as he listened to John's proposal. "He can't fucking play at right-back — he's never a right-back," Jack protested. But he was eventually talked round and put me in on the right-hand side of defence. I thought I had a good game in a 3-0 win and Jack let me continue in the side during Blackhall's absence. I took to playing at right-back straight away because I could see the whole picture.

In one of my first games at right-back, we played Grimsby and they had a big, lanky lad on the left-wing called Paul Emson, who was very quick. Jack was worried about him, but I had a great game against him, never giving him a kick. Jack came up to me at the end of the game and said, "Fantastic game today son, absolutely superb." I carried on at right-back from then on. It was amazing how quickly the tables turned because after getting stick as a midfield player, just a month or two later the fans were chanting "Zico" and they absolutely loved me to death.

One of the trickiest wingers I came up against when I was still learning the ropes at right-back was a young Chris Waddle. He came to Hillsborough with Newcastle, not long after coming out of the sausage factory where he worked before becoming a professional footballer. You knew Waddle was going to go all the way in the game even then because he'd got everything. He was absolutely taking the piss with his trickery on the wing and when we came in at half-time, Jack Charlton told me in no uncertain terms that he wasn't happy. "You big fat cunt, are you going to fucking boot him or am I going to take you off?" he said. I didn't want to go off so in the second half I booted Waddle and he never got a kick from then on. Jack was obviously satisfied with what I had done because he didn't carry out his threat to substitute me.

I tangled with Chelsea hard man Micky Droy when I was a youngster. I went down the line and as he went to clear the ball, I went over the top and really did him. He was one of their most important players because he won everything, so I was pleased, thinking to myself that he wasn't going to come back on. I couldn't believe it when he came back on after having about five or six stitches in his shin. I never went near him after that because he was a giant of a bloke. Fortunately, he didn't come after me so he must have just thought it was an accident.

As well as carrying out my defensive duties, I was also scoring goals and making a hell of a lot of goals. I'd had to go backwards to progress and I was delighted with the way things had turned out. After starting out as a centre-forward at school, I'd played in midfield before finally settling at right-back. I was going further and further backwards and I think if I hadn't made it as a defender, I'd have probably been a ball-boy!

CHAPTER FIVE

The Flying Pig Takes Off

Jack Charlton was a great character who signed the players he wanted for Sheffield Wednesday and did well for the club. He could be a bit forgetful at times and regularly forgot the names of players. I can remember him once naming a team with 12 players in it! After somebody pointed it out, he just pointed to John Pearson and said, "It's all right – Pearson, you're not playing."

On the training ground, Jack would take free-kicks with his shoes on and still find the net on a regular basis. Some players struggle to manage that with their boots on but Jack would come over – with a fag hanging down in the corner of his mouth – and say, "This is how to do it." With his brogues on, he'd bend the ball round the wall and put it into the top corner, leaving all of us looking at each other in amazement.

Boozing, Betting & Brawling

Jack was a funny, funny guy. He used to really get into players and he'd pick his fights. I can remember once when he had one of his bust-ups with Terry Curran, who was our star player. It was freezing cold weather and there was snow on the ground, so the training ground was out of use, forcing us to go inside and use the gym. Something went off between Jack and Terry and all of a sudden, Jack was wrestling with his sheepskin coat, trying to get it off, calling Terry a "long-haired fucker". Terry was having a go back, wanting to fight him. I don't know what it was over, whether Jack had said he wasn't playing in a game or if Terry had said he was crap at what he was doing, but it was so funny seeing a player want to fight the manager. Some of the players were holding Terry back and others were holding Jack. A few of them were saying, "Go on, let them go, let them have a fight." John Harris came into the gym, saw the commotion and said, "What's blummin' going off?" That was typical of John because he never used to swear. Jack and Terry eventually calmed down and shook hands.

Terry was the main man at the time. He was a great character who loved a gamble and he and Andy McCulloch had the worst greyhounds in the world. When I was injured on one occasion, I went to see physio John Honey in midweek for some treatment. Terry and Andy came into the treatment room to have a word with John and the next thing I knew, I was being ushered off the treatment bench after being told it was needed. I was expecting a player to come into the room – probably a senior one – but to my amazement, Terry and Andy brought in this greyhound! "We've got to treat this dog because it's running on Friday night," said John. I watched as they lifted the dog, called "Spiral Please", onto the bench and used the ultrasound equipment on it! I couldn't believe what I was seeing. I thought, "These are taking the piss here, all they're bothered about is a fucking greyhound". But they were senior pros and I was just a kid, so I didn't argue; I just left them to it. All the players backed Spiral Please when it ran and I think it finished last.

Terry was also on the scene when I travelled with the squad to London for a game, soon after getting into the first-team. We travelled down to the hotel on the Friday afternoon, had an evening meal and then killed some time mixing together in the hotel. I got in the lift with Terry and Ian Mellor and went down to the bar area. I noticed some birds stood at the bar and I was told they were prostitutes, so I tapped Terry on the shoulder and said, "Terry, lend us fifty quid."

"You what?" he replied.

"Lend us fifty quid."

"What for?"

"One of those prostitutes down there," I said, pointing to where the girls were stood.

"Shut up," he said, "I'll get you one of them for nowt later."

He never produced, though. Terry's never forgotten that incident because he still recounts the story now when I see him.

Jack Charlton's lad, Peter, used to travel to some of the away games and stay in the hotel with us. He was only a young lad, probably about 14 or 15, but he used to smoke and drink and was street-wise. He'd knock on your door and

Boozing, Betting & Brawling

come into the room for a drink and a fag. He'd get to the mini-bar, take out a miniature vodka bottle, pour the drink into a glass and then fill the bottle with water! He'd do the same with Bacardi, which is also clear. The first time I saw him do that, I was thinking to myself what a good idea it was. Then I had second thoughts for a moment. "Hang on," I said, "we're going to get charged for that."

"No problem," Peter assured me, "they don't check. As soon as they see that the bottle is full, they're not bothered."

Once he'd put the bottle full of water back in the fridge, he'd drink the vodka. I was gobsmacked because I'd never seen that scam before. After that, I used to do the same trick myself when we stayed in hotels. I'd take out a can of Coke, which I paid for, and drink all the vodka free of charge. It worked all the time but you can't do it now because the drinks are on sensors. As soon as you lift a bottle or can off the shelf, it activates a sensor to tell the hotel people that it's been taken. They've probably been ripped off so many times in the past by people like me and Peter Charlton!

Ante Mirocevic, who was a nice guy and a good footballer, could hardly speak any English and I couldn't believe it when they gave him some English books and told him to room with me. It used to piss me off, having to listen to him trying to get to grips with the language. Once I was sat on the bed watching telly and he was tapping me on the shoulder saying, "Melly, this is a radiator," pointing at one of his books. I'd look at the book and say, "Yes, that is a radiator." When I'd had enough and wanted to go to sleep, I'd say, "Ante, this is a pillow, fucking sleep." The penny would finally drop and he'd get in his bed.

Listening to Ante could also be funny at times. When some hostages were shown on the TV, he said, "Oh, sausages." Well I just burst out laughing and said, "No, Ante, no sausages." I got him to say "fuck off" and "wanker" which was so funny to hear him say because he didn't know what he was saying. He used to be telling everybody to "fuck off". Ante had a bubble car and he looked so funny, with his hairy face and bald head, when he was driving it. The lads used to take the piss out of him but Ante was so proud of the car, treating it as though it was a Rolls-Royce. Ante never used to wear shin pads when he was playing and he used to have his socks rolled down, which was a licence to boot him.

It was Jack Charlton who called me "The Flying Pig". We were due to travel to QPR and it was an overnight stop, so we were setting off on the Friday. On the way to Hillsborough, I went to the bookies to put a bet on and didn't realise what time it was. When I got to the ground, the team coach had gone and I thought, "Fucking hell fire, I'm going to get a right bollocking here, I'm going to get a fine and everything". A guy called Frank Ashton, who was a physio for Middlewood Rovers, was waiting at the ground and I went over to him and told him what had happened. "Frank, you're going to have to take me down to QPR," I said. He agreed to do it and said that we should be able to catch up with the team coach on the M1. We got into Frank's car and he put his foot down on the pedal as soon as we got on the motorway. When we finally caught up with the coach, Frank flashed his lights to indicate to the driver to pull over. I got on the coach and all the players were looking at me, but Jack Charlton didn't say a thing.

When we arrived at the hotel and then had something to eat, some of the lads left bits of food on their plate, which I picked up and ate. Jack saw me eating the left-overs and coupled with the fact that I'd "flown" down the M1 to catch up with the coach, he decided to nick-name me "The Flying Pig". We beat QPR 1-0 the next day and Jack's decision to not fine me for missing the coach was probably down to the fact that we won. That match was an experience because it was when QPR had their plastic pitch. Jack didn't want us to pass the ball on it. He just said, "Boot the fucking ball as high as you can and you'll get a result from this game." If we got a free-kick around the half-way line, one of the players had to flick it and another would have to boot it up in the air. It was embarrassing really, but it was effective because if teams went there to try and play football, they got murdered.

Jack's assistant was Maurice Setters and he was a hard man who took no prisoners. He used to point his finger in your face when he was giving you a bollocking. Former Liverpool star Ian St John, who later became a successful TV presenter, also had a spell on the coaching staff. I can remember him having a go at me because I didn't run after a ball in a practice match. He must have run half the length of the field and kicked me straight up the arse before shouting, "You idle bastard, when you're playing 11-a-side you've got to run back, so you fucking run back in a five-a-side game." It bucked my ideas up and I ran back all the time after that.

There were a couple of birds who used to hang around the training ground, waiting for players. They were like groupies and everyone shagged them. They were from a place not far from the training ground called Wadsley Bridge, so they became known as the "Wadsleys". The in-place to go to at that time was Josephine's Nightclub and the Wadsleys used to go there as well. You could guarantee that they'd finish up going home with players at the end of the night. We were in Josephine's one night when John Pearson went home with one of the Wadsleys.

She was a big, fat, horrible bird and when I say horrible, she was horrible. I left it for a couple of weeks before deciding to wind up John in training one day. I told Charlie Williamson about what I was planning to do and he agreed to back me up. We were about to finish training when I went over to John and started on him. "John, you know that bird you've been with, one of the Wadsleys?" I said.

"How do you know about that?" he replied, surprised that his secret had got out.

"I saw your name int' book," I said. I'd regularly have a laugh with the other players, telling them that I'd seen their name in the signing-in book at the house of one of the girls.

"Ha, ha, very funny," he said, just laughing it off.

"Well, you won't be laughing in a minute," I continued.

"Why?" he said, suddenly interested to find out what I was on about.

Boozing, Betting & Brawling

"She's pregnant."

"You what?"

"She's just told me."

I've never seen somebody's mood change so quickly. One minute he was laughing and joking and the next minute the colour had drained from his face and he looked devastated. I didn't ease up – despite the fact that he was obviously very worried by this time – and I started making the shape of a bump over my stomach with my hand. It was the day before a game and Jack Charlton got us all together at the end of training to tell us who was in the side. Big Jack looked over at John and clearly realised straight away from his deathly white face that something was troubling him. "What's up, John?" he said, "you look as though you've put someone in the family way!" Me and Charlie Williamson looked at each other and burst out laughing. John was sweating and he just didn't know what to do. I felt sorry for him after a while, but I'd started it and had to carry on the pretence for a bit longer before telling him.

We reached the semi-finals of the FA Cup in 1983 after thrashing Burnley 5-0 in a quarter-final replay. We were the favourites in the semi-final because we were doing well in the league, but it was a disaster. In practice matches leading up to the game, Charlie Williamson had been playing at left-back and Pat Heard was in midfield. But on the day of the game, Jack suddenly decided to change the team, leaving Charlie Williamson out and putting Pat Heard at left-back. Ante Mirocevic, or "Microwave" as we used to call him, came into midfield.

Mel STERLAND

The day didn't get off to a good start because we left Heard and David Mills at the hotel. We got on the bus, travelled to Highbury and when we were in the dressing room, someone realised there were two players missing. Heard and Mills had to get a taxi from the hotel. Even in the dressing room it was a farce because Mirocevic was hanging out of the window, looking at all the fans to try and find his family so he could give them their tickets.

As I ran out at Highbury, I looked to my right where the Wednesday fans were and saw this big flag with "Zico" written on it. I think it was some lads off the Manor who'd had the flag made. Fans had started calling me Zico after the Brazilian who starred in the 1982 World Cup. Like me, he took free-kicks and had long, flowing hair.

It was a disaster of a game because we didn't play well and I felt sorry for all the supporters who went down there. After Jimmy Case gave Brighton the lead with a free-kick, Ante Mirocevic got a great equaliser, only for Michael Robinson to score Brighton's winner. I punched the ball into the net after going to cover the goalkeeper, so it would have been a penalty if it had gone wide.

Jack Charlton decided to step down in the summer of 1983 after six years in the job because he thought he'd taken the club as far as he could. I was sad to see Jack go, because he was a great guy, but I think he got out at the right time.

Things were changing for me away from football as well because me and Charmaine, who later became my wife, had just moved into our first house together. It was a big step, but I'd just been given a new three-year contract, so

Boozing, Betting & Brawling

we went and bought a nice little semi-detached house in the Chapeltown area of Sheffield. Charmaine was only 16 when we first met in 1978 at a football presentation night she attended with her brothers. One of her brothers, Tony James, played for Leicester City. He was a big centre-half, who was about to sign for Tottenham when he suffered a broken leg. Her other brother, Chris, played for Scarborough.

When Charmaine was about 19, I drove past her when she was out shopping, pipped my horn at her and she waved back. It was her legs I remembered; she had the longest legs in the world. I later bumped into her at Romeo & Juliet's Nightclub in Sheffield when I went up to her in the queue and asked her if she was going into the club. When we were inside the club, I went over to chat to her and then we danced. We started going out together in December 1982 and moved in together five months later.

When me and Charmaine went on holiday to Cyprus that summer, we used to find letters pushed under the door of our hotel room from the president of the local football club, urging me to sign for them. There was no mention of the sort of money on offer, but he said we'd be given a car and a six-bedroom house. Every other day there would be a letter there waiting when we got back to our room. I assume the president was alerted to the fact I was staying there by one of the hotel staff because I handed my passport in at the hotel reception and it stated on it that I was a professional footballer. I wasn't tempted to move because everything was going well at Wednesday then.

While I was in Cyprus, the Sheffield Wednesday board had to look for a new manager to build on the foundations Jack Charlton had laid. The man they appointed went on to have a huge influence on my career.

CHAPTER SIX

"It's A Man, It's A Man!"

I was still on holiday when Howard Wilkinson was named as Sheffield Wednesday's new manager. I found out when I phoned up my dad to ask him who'd got the job. I must admit that the news took me by surprise because Howard wasn't well-known then, but he turned out to be a great manager.

Howard is from Sheffield and he was a Wednesday supporter before playing for the club. He'd managed Boston United at non-league level before impressing at Notts County. A lot of people think that Howard is quite a dour character, but he's good at weighing people up and I found him to be great.

When Howard came to Wednesday, he worked us a lot harder than Jack had done, running the balls off us! That meant that we were fit and organised. Players usually finish training at 12 o'clock on a Friday, but we used to be there until about quarter to three, working on set-pieces and organisation. It was unbelievable, but it got us results because everyone knew what they were doing.

We used to run round Derwent Valley. I wasn't the best runner, but Martin Hodge was worse than me. There were times when a tractor went by and you'd jump on it to have a breather. I think "Wilko" got wise to us cheating, so he told his assistant, Peter Eustace, to keep an eye on us. Coach Mick Hennigan also made sure we didn't take any short-cuts. Wilko had Eustace at one place and Hennigan at another.

During one run, we'd all set off and after a while I looked back to see big, fat keepers Iain Hesford and Martin Hodge both behind me, along with Carl Bradshaw. Then after running round a bend, I looked ahead and saw Hesford, Hodge and Bradshaw all in front of me. The sneaky bastards had managed to take a short-cut across the canal because the water was low! I was left trailing in last, looking a right twat. Wilko wasn't happy with me and Eustace and Hennigan also made their feelings known because Bradshaw was crap at running and Hesford was even worse. "Hezzy" was a fatty who didn't like those scales, just like I didn't. I was in the shit for that while "Brad" and Hezzy were laughing their bollocks off.

There was a time when Tony Cunningham got hopelessly lost during a run. Tony had not been at the club long so he was unfamiliar with the area where we were running. After finding himself detached from the main pack of runners, Tony ran round a bend and caught site of a yellow jersey, which he took to be one of the keepers, Martin Hodge or Iain Hesford. He caught up with the yellow

Boozing, Betting & Brawling

jersey and found that it wasn't Hodgey or Hezzy, it was a road worker digging a hole, wearing a fluorescent jacket! The rest of the players were nowhere to be seen and Tony had no idea how to get back to where we were being picked up, so he had to be given a lift by a friendly farmer who found us waiting in the mini-bus at the car park.

Tony is now a solicitor in Lincoln. He was always a bright lad and you knew he'd do well for himself after finishing with football. He turns out now and again in charity games I'm involved with and he's still as fit as anything.

Simon Stainrod was overweight – even fatter than me – when he first came to Hillsborough, so Wilko used to make him run round the perimeter of the pitch. He had him in morning and afternoon and Stainrod ended up losing about two stone after Wilko got hold of him. "Stan" used to play cards with us on a Friday night before away games and he had a big fat wallet, full of money. But I could guarantee that when we got back to Sheffield, he'd have no money left. That was because he was the worst card player ever – he used to lose all the time. We called him "Billy Big Time" because he used to strut around.

With the training being so tough, players would get out of it if they could. I remember a time when Mark Chamberlain rang the club doctor to say he was ill and couldn't get in for training. Wilko, being the shrewd guy he is, knew "Chambo" had probably been out on the piss the night before, so he sent the doctor round to his house. The doctor was knocking on Chambo's door, but there was no sign of him. It then emerged that he was playing snooker in a club round the corner from his house and he got fined when he came in the next day.

Mel STERLAND

If we didn't have a game, we were worked extra hard in training. There were a couple of times when Wilko took us for a seven-mile run after the pitch was frozen over on a Friday, only for the weather to improve the next day, so they got the sprinklers on the pitch to get the game called off because we were knackered!

Howard encouraged me to get forward as much as possible, so I'd regularly bomb upfield, get crosses in and score goals. We'd got a good defence with the likes of Micky Lyons, Mark Smith and Nigel Worthington, which made it easy for me. They'd say, "Go on, keep bombing on."

Micky Lyons was a great professional who used to get carried away with his pre-match warm-ups. He'd get a forward to stand in front of him and someone had to chuck the ball over the forward, so Micky could head it back. I remember one time when John Pearson was the player used and he never ducked, so Micky head-butted his head and had to have about six stitches put in around his eye. He just went into the treatment room, said to the doctor, "Stitch me up" and then when that was done he went back on the pitch.

Another time Micky was "stitched up" was when we told him that we were going out in fancy dress – and he turned up dressed as a caveman. When we met up in Henry's, which was a trendy wine bar in the centre of Sheffield, all the lads had a collar and tie on and Micky turned up wearing this caveman outfit, complete with a big wig, carrying a large bone. He looked a right twat! I don't think anyone thought that Micky would fall for it when he was told that everyone was going out in fancy dress. We were inside Henry's when a taxi pulled up outside and Micky got out of it in his outfit. When he saw the rest of us dressed normally, he whacked us all with this bone which he'd picked up from a butcher's shop. We all copped for it and then Micky just carried on with enjoying himself because he loved a drink. Micky's a great bloke and he did really well for Wednesday.

Up front we had Lee Chapman, who did well for us. He should give me some of the money he's got now because I used to make all his goals for him! Every time I crossed the ball, Chapman got his head to it. He was very brave – if there were boots flying, "Chappy" used to get his head in.

I used to room with a player who was the dirtiest footballer I've ever known. He just used to look around for women when we were in a hotel preparing for an away match. I can remember rooming with him once when I got back to the room as drunk as a lord and he was in bed with this bird. He told me to get out and I said, "Fuck off, you can get out with her." I think he'd done what he wanted to do with her because he booted her out.

Nobody wanted to room with me because I used to sleep-walk and talk in my sleep. One room-mate said that in the middle of the night I jumped up and shouted, "Wake up, wake up, there's a monkey in the corner." I made him get up and go to the back of the chair in the corner of the room to see if there was a monkey there.

We won promotion to the First Division at the end of Wilko's first season in charge, finishing level on points with champions Chelsea and just missing out on the title on goal-difference. I scored a crucial penalty against Grimsby

Mel STERLAND

towards the end of the season. I think it was Gary Megson who knocked the ball through to Tony Cunningham who went over in the area, winning a penalty. I don't think it was a penalty, to be honest, but the referee gave it. Nigel Batch was the goalkeeper and I remember him messing about on the line, trying to put me off. I managed to block that out, putting the ball to his left.

We secured promotion a week later, with four games still to go, beating Crystal Palace 1-0 at home and I was the match-winner again from the penalty spot. Cunningham won the penalty as before and I can remember taking that spot-kick as if it was yesterday, putting it to the keeper's left in front of the Kop.

It was a memorable year for me, both professionally and personally. As well as scoring the goal which took us up, I played for the England Under-21s and my daughter Chantelle was born. That was superb because having a kid opens your eyes. My dad, who liked a flutter and was generally quite lucky with his bets, won £3,000 and insisted on buying a pram for Chantelle out of his winnings. Chantelle went to matches from nine months old and she'd recognise me as I ran out onto the pitch, going crazy, sat on Charmaine's knee, waving her arms around. It was different when our son Nathan was born a couple of years later because he never showed the slightest bit of interest in football. He used to take his toys to matches to keep himself occupied whereas Chantelle loves football and goes to the games with me now.

I went to a PFA dinner in London, along with a few other Wednesday players. At that time you didn't have to show your room card or anything when you wanted to put drinks on your room, you just gave them a name. There was a

Boozing, Betting & Brawling

real arrogant bastard who turned up in the bar, flashing his wealth. Someone overheard him when he said his name and room number after he'd ordered some drinks, so we all put our food and drinks on his room! Everyone was at it. We were ordering steak sandwiches, bottles of lager and then bottles of champagne. I think Gary Megson ordered a bottle of brandy. It all went on this guy's room and he must have had a heart attack when he got his bill!

Howard Wilkinson took all the players and their wives on a pre-season trip to Keswick in the Lake District. All the women had a good piss-up while we were running up mountains. Martin Hodge was known as "Bulldog Bollocks", so we got a big banana and arranged it, along with two massive plums, on his plate when he came down for breakfast!

My first game in the top-flight was on the opening day of the season when Nottingham Forest came to Hillsborough. John Robertson was playing for Forest and after I booted him, he asked me how many medals I'd got and how much I earned a week. I was only young and I'd never heard that before, so I was honest and said, "I've got nowt and I'm overdrawn at the bank." I had the last laugh though because we beat them and I scored a penalty. When the referee blew the final whistle, I went straight over to Robertson and said, "Well, I've got my win bonus going in now, what have you got out of this game?"

We continued to make good progress under Wilko that season, finishing in eighth place. We also had a decent run in the League Cup, reaching the fifth round before losing to Chelsea in a second replay. The first replay was an epic 4-4 draw at Hillsborough. We were 3-0 up at half-time and absolutely cruising,

Mel STERLAND

but it all changed after Chelsea brought on Paul Canoville. I was marking him and he caused all sorts of problems, running me daft as Chelsea stormed back to lead 4-3. With the seconds ticking away, we were awarded a penalty. After knocking the ball past their left-back, Doug Rougvie, I just fell over and couldn't believe it when the ref pointed to the spot. Andy Blair should have taken the penalty because he'd taken three against Luton in the previous round and scored all three, but he bottled it. I don't know if it was because Mickey Thomas had stuck one on him. It was some punch as well, a good left hook. Mickey later told me, "He said something which wound me up, so I had to smack him." When we'd played down at Stamford Bridge, Thomas and Blair were having a right go at each other. Mickey went over to Andy and said, "I've shagged your wife." He hadn't, as it turned out, he'd just said it to get into Andy's head. It obviously worked because Andy was thinking, "Has he shagged my wife?" When we got the penalty, I turned to Andy and said, "Come on then, son." But he said, "I can't take it, you better take it." He wasn't having a good game, but then again neither was I because Canoville had come on and taken the piss. But I put the ball down on the spot with only seconds to go and smashed it through the keeper's legs to make it 4-4.

When the final whistle blew, Rougvie came up to me and he was absolutely livid, calling me a "fat, lying, cheating bastard" and everything. He absolutely slaughtered me. When I went home and watched the highlights on TV, the camera showed me and Rougvie speaking to each other as we walked off and the commentator said, "Isn't it nice to see two fellow professionals talking about the game." If only he knew what Rougvie was saying!

In the summer of 1985, we went to Thailand to play Watford in a game being shown live on TV over there. It ended 0-0 and was the worst game ever. It absolutely pissed it down and you couldn't play football in those conditions. One night we went out in Bangkok and there were transsexuals everywhere. Everybody fancied them because they were absolutely gorgeous. They'd be playing with your cock under the table and it was like living in a different world. A couple of well-known players went off with these men/women and took them back to their hotel room. The day after, everyone wanted to know what had happened with them. All the lads were saying, "Did you shag 'em then?" That was when the truth came out. One of them was apparently kissing this "bird" on the bed and the other two were in the bathroom. The player on the bed put his hand down "her" skirt and found a cock! He then jumped up and shouted: "****, ****, it's a man, it's a man!" The other player rushed out of the bathroom with the intention of smacking the man/woman, who responded by reaching into a bag, pulling out a knife and cutting him on his chest. It wasn't a bad gash, but the blade made a mark across his chest. The player then turned round and chinned the other one who was obviously also a man. When the player in question got home, I think he told his wife that the scar on his chest was as a result of being caught by a high tackle during the match in Thailand! It was a load of bollocks because there were no tackles in the game.

Another player went out for a drink on his own while me and the rest of the players were in the hotel, having a few drinks before going out. The player who'd gone out on his own came back to the hotel, sweating like a rapist. "What's up?" we asked him.

"Fucking hell, I can't fucking believe that," he said.

"Why, what's happened?"

"I'm walking down the street and I've seen this bird, she's told me to fucking come in, so I went in and shagged her and she wants fucking paying. She's threatened to set these bouncers on to me so I got out of there as quick as I could."

He wasn't the quickest player, but I don't think he was found wanting for pace on that occasion! We told him not to sit down with us in case the bouncers from the brothel he'd been in came looking for the money he owed, so he went upstairs to his room. Nothing was said about the incident after that, but when we came back to England, it turned out that the prostitute the player had been with had given him a dose! His knob and balls were red-raw and nobody would get into the bath with him, fearing they'd catch what he'd picked up. I think he told his missus he'd got kicked in the bollocks playing football. The club doctor eventually sorted out the problem with some Penicillin.

I can remember Howard Wilkinson coming into the dressing room at half-time in a match, ranting and raving despite the fact we were winning 2-0. "You fucking bunch of twats, if you put in a performance like that you'll get fucking beaten," he shouted. He then threw a cup which bounced up and hit my knee. I bit my lip because I didn't want to show that it had hurt me, but I had to come off in the second half because my knee had swollen up. I've seen Wilko throw all sorts of things and even pick up benches when he's been angry.

Howard once smacked John Pearson because he wanted him to harden up. John was soft – we called him "Big Emu" – and defenders used to bully him. He never used to say anything when they tried to intimidate him. Wilko had a habit of pointing a finger at you to get a reaction and he went up to John after one game, had a go at him and smacked him across the face. Wilko wanted a reaction from John, but he just laughed at him.

When I was playing, there used to be fights all the time in training and I don't think that was a bad thing at all because it showed that we cared. Players now hand transfer requests in if they've been involved in a fight with a team-mate. Imre Varadi regularly had a fight and I remember a time when he had a real scrap with Chris Morris. After Wilko set up a "tiggy" game in training with a ball and players inside a circle, Imre and Chris both went for the ball at the same time. I turned round to see them fighting over the ball, knocking the shit out of each other. On another occasion, Imre had a fight with Nigel Worthington during a five-a-side game. Wilko just left them to get on with it because he loved it when players had a go at each other. Imre was so competitive and that was how Howard liked it.

He's a character, Imre. There was a time when we went to Ireland and it was clear that something was troubling him. Imre was a very fit guy, but Iain Hesford and Martin Hodge were beating him at running. Wilko thought he was injured, but he wasn't. Imre was rooming with me and I said, "Fucking hell, Razor, goalkeepers are beating you at running – what's up?" He insisted there was nothing wrong, but I didn't believe him. On the way home, I asked him again and this time he told me the truth. "I've split up with the missus," he said, "we've fallen out with each other." Before he went to his house, I told him there was nothing to worry about, but he couldn't even get in because she'd changed all the locks. A taxi pulled up at my house and he got out with all his cases. He asked if he could stay for a month or so and he ended up staying for six months. His missus didn't like it because she thought he should be on the streets, but I said to him, "Tell your missus to fuck off."

Martin Hodge had got a bit of a temper and he'd flare-up quicker than most. Tony Cunningham played for Barnsley against Wednesday just before signing for us and he remembers Hodgey being funny with him when he first arrived at the club. Hodgey wouldn't even speak to Cunningham for the first couple of weeks because he'd clattered into him in that game.

I had several run-ins with Hodgey during our time together at Hillsborough. One incident was before a game at QPR. We were having a game of cards in my room the night before the game and I had a big cold sore on my face. Hodgey ordered a glass of Coca-Cola on my room and I forgot all about it. Next morning, I went downstairs and said to Martin, "Look Hodgey, have you paid for that Coke you had in my room?" Hodgey, who never swore, said, "Why don't you flippin' shut up you flippin' fat get" and put his finger on my cold sore, making it bleed. Hodgey used to give people kidney punches for a laugh and I'd had a few off him, probably the week before. So after making my cold sore bleed, I thought I'd give him something back. I'd got a pair of astro-boots

Boozing, Betting & Brawling

in my hand, which I was going to wear on the plastic pitch at Loftus Road, so I whacked Hodgey on the head with them. As I did it, Wilko was walking past and he just winked at me. "Fucking come on then," Hodgey said to me. "Look Hodgey, go away or I'll make a mess of you," I replied. But he refused to back down and was still having a go at me. Then he came up close to me, put his face in mine and said, "Right, you flippin' fat get." So I nutted him…just as Wilko walked past. I expected to get a bollocking from Wilko, but he just winked at me again!

A lot of players were scared of Howard Wilkinson, but he knew the players he could bollock and the ones he had to put an arm around. He definitely got the best out of me. It was Howard who made me aware of my defensive duties and improved my defending.

My weight was a problem, so Wilko put it in my contract that I'd get fined £100 for each pound over my playing weight of 13 stone and two pounds. We used to get weighed on a Friday, play on the Saturday and then go out on Saturday night. I'd get up on Sunday, take laxatives and water tablets and go for a run ahead of the weigh-in on Monday. I also used to run wearing a plastic bag over my training kit on a Sunday to sweat it off.

I was lucky to escape a big fine after one weekend when I over-did things. Charmaine cooked a meal on the Friday night, we went to Josephine's Nightclub for a meal after the game on Saturday and then we went out for Sunday lunch with the rest of the family. When I was weighed on Monday, I found that I'd put seven pounds on. I should have had a £700 fine, but Wilko let me off because we'd won on the Saturday and I'd scored.

When we went on a three-week holiday to America, I had to run every day to make sure that I wasn't over my weight limit when I got back. There would be an all-you-can-eat buffet and I used to be up at the crack of dawn, running it off. I worried about my weight so much when I was playing and that's why I don't bother now.

I was one of those who could go out drinking and then get up and train the next day. Howard took the view that if it didn't affect your performance, he'd turn a blind eye. But as soon as it did affect your performance, he'd be on your case straight away. There was one time when Mick Hennigan and Peter Eustace came into Josephine's Nightclub because Wilko had heard the players were out when they shouldn't have been. Hennigan and Eustace found us in there and sent us home.

Wilko was a very disciplined manager. Sometimes he'd send you home if you were late for training, but if you did the business for him, he looked after you. Two particular occasions when I needed his help stand out in my mind. One was when I thought I had a life-threatening disease and the other was when I had money worries which threatened to spiral out of control. Howard came to my aid on both occasions and I'll always be grateful to him for that.

CHAPTER SEVEN

Health And Money Worries

"I think I've got cancer", I said to Charmaine. The way I said it, she thought it had been confirmed and she was worried sick until I put her straight and told her that it was only what I thought. The reason why I'd convinced myself I was dying of the disease was that I lost about two stone inside about a month. It got to the stage where I'd go home after training, collapse on the floor and start throwing up.

I spoke to Howard Wilkinson about my fears and he was fantastic, immediately arranging for me to see the best specialist available. After undergoing a series of tests – which cost the club about £3,000 – I was told that there was nothing wrong with me physically. The specialist put my dramatic weight-loss down to anxiety as it was around the anniversary of my mum dying.

Mel STERLAND

Howard also helped me when I told him I was having trouble looking after my finances. I used to get into all sorts of scrapes with money because I'd just spend whatever I had. And I never worried about spending all my money because I just used to think about the next win bonus. Most of the money went on gambling and I was in trouble because I'd be left with no money to pay the bills. Howard was very understanding and put me in touch with an accountant called Bob Grierson, who is now Sheffield Wednesday's financial director. I went along to see Bob and after chatting he worked out what I needed to live on. My wages went to Bob and he took out the money required to cover the mortgage on my house, along with the various household expenses, and then told me how much was left to spend. I had to go to Bob's office, which was near to the Children's Hospital in Sheffield, to get cheques from him. As a further safe-guard, Howard had to counter-sign the cheques. It was like being a kid again, receiving pocket money! It was a good job that someone was looking after the money side of things because I would have just done the lot in.

I used to pick up Carl Shutt and take him to training when we were at Wednesday. He used to stink of chip pan fat, which used to do my box in. Carl Bradshaw, who later played for Sheffield United, also used to travel with us when he was an apprentice. I used to have him on about the fact that he couldn't read. I'd tell him that I'd only give him a lift if he could read a certain word I picked out on a sign or whatever. "Shut up Mel," he'd say, "stop taking the piss out of me." I remember seeing a white van with the word "maintenance" written on the side. Pointing to the van, I said, "What's it say then, Brads?"

Boozing, Betting & Brawling

"Main entrance," he said. I was laughing that much that I nearly crashed the car!

Another time we were travelling to Ladybower reservoir for a long run organised by Howard Wilkinson. There was a sign at the side of the water, which included the word "dangerous". I thought I'd have a bit of fun at Carl's expense again. "Come on then Brad, what's that say?"

"Easy," he said, apparently confident that he knew what it was, "it's dan-ger-oos." Everybody in the car was laughing their head off. "You're bastards, you lot, taking the piss out of me," Carl said. Brads was a big Sheffield United fan but I don't think anyone at Wednesday knew that at the time. I'd have given him plenty of stick about it if I'd have known, I can assure you. Carl and his brother Darren, who played for Newcastle, are both great lads. They're in the building trade now. Carl's a brickie and Darren's an electrician. I was Carl's Best Man when he got married.

On one occasion when I was injured, Brads was also receiving treatment and the physio, Alan Smith, took us to the gym for a work-out. After doing the weights and using the various machines in the gym, we had to rest for a while. Carl spotted some boxing gloves on the floor of the gym and decided that he wanted to fight. That wasn't the best idea considering the fact that we were both trying to get fit for a game the following Saturday. "Come on then, fucking big-headed cunt, let's see how tha can box," he said.

"Sit down daft twat or I'll fucking knock thee out," I replied.

"Come on then," he said, throwing a pair of boxing gloves to me and then putting a pair on himself. He came towards me, moving his body about like boxers do and holding up his gloved fists. I just aimed one punch, smacking him straight on the nose. He fell straight down and his eyes rolled to the back of his head, leaving me thinking I'd killed him for a split second, but he soon came round. As Carl was about to get to his feet, Alan Smith came into the gym and went barmy when he saw what we'd been doing. Alan would get really mad if he saw you messing about when you were injured. Nobody wanted to be injured because "Smithy" was really strict and he'd work you really hard to get you fit. Before Alan came to the club, people would read newspapers in the treatment room but that stopped when he was brought in. "It's a treatment room and not a doss house," is what he used to say. Terry Curran and Andy McCulloch wouldn't have got away with taking a greyhound into the treatment room under Smithy! That would have been a no-go because you couldn't even go in there with your shoes on.

Smithy was the victim of a practical joke from Iain Hesford. Hezzy, who was a great keeper and a funny lad, went into the treatment room one day, shit on a plate and put it in a drawer! Smithy didn't know where the hell this horrible smell was coming from. He saw the joke when he eventually discovered the "present" Hesford had left for him and had a laugh about it.

Hezzy loved a drink and never used to stay in. He lived at the back of the Middlewood Tavern, which is not far from Wednesday's training ground, so that was one of his regular pubs. After going there one Friday night for a few pints – despite the fact that he was in the squad for the game the following day

Boozing, Betting & Brawling

— he was caught by Peter Eustace. "What are you doing here at this time?" Eustace asked him.

"I'm house-hunting," Hezzy replied.

"What do you mean?"

"I'm looking for a house."

"Well, you won't find any fucking houses here, will you?"

Lawrie Madden looked just like a tramp when he first arrived at Hillsborough, but he turned out to be an astute signing. He'd got a scruffy beard and had a long black coat on when he turned up during pre-season training. He just came into the changing room, sat down and we were all looking at each other, wondering who he was. Peter Eustace turned to him and said, "Can I help you?" When Lawrie explained that he'd come for a trial, nobody could believe it because he looked so scruffy. Howard Wilkinson knew him from their time together at Boston and he impressed on trial and went on to do ever so well for Wednesday.

Lawrie used to get some stick. When he wanted you to push forward, he'd urge you to "come up". With Lawrie's southern accent, however, it sounded more like "cam ap", so we'd mimic him, shouting, "Cam ap, cam ap." Gary Megson and Gary Shelton were brilliant at it and they murdered him. But one day when Lawrie wasn't there, Wilko pulled us up in the dressing room and said, "Look, I know you're having a laugh, but you're going too far with this cam ap business." So we had to stop because Lawrie was getting the hump. Lawrie's so tight, he only breathes in! An example of that was when we were on tour in

Mel STERLAND

Spain. It was Charlie Williamson's round and everyone was on San Migel – apart from Hodgey who was on coffee because he never used to drink – and then Lawrie pipes up and says, "I'll have a treble Baileys."

Nigel Worthington was a great signing who also did well when he later went to Leeds. I only ever saw one player go by him quite often and that was Gordon Strachan. Gordon used to give him a torrid time, but I never saw anyone else really trouble him. When we went out on a Christmas do one year, we ended up in Josephine's Nightclub, which was full of mirrors. Nigel told us that he was going and we said goodnight to him, but he was still in the club an hour later because he couldn't get out of the place due to the mirrors!

Another important player for us at that time was Gary Megson. He used to come in at half-time and puke his guts up with nerves and once even did it on the pitch.

Carl Shutt, who worked as an engineer while playing non-league football, was a character. He'd just signed for Wednesday from Spalding when we set him up. Lee Chapman rang him up and pretended to be a journalist called David Walker. "It's David Walker from *The Sun*," Chappy said, putting on a different voice, "we'd like to do a piece with you. Could we set something up at the training ground?" Shutty said, "Is it possible you could ring back tomorrow because it's all new to me and I want to check it out with the lads." When he came in for training, he told me and a few others what had happened and asked what he should do. I told him to ask for five hundred quid and then Chapman added, "Ask him for five hundred, but no cheques – it's got to be cash and you can put it straight into the players' pool." Chapman rang him two or three hours later and said, "It's David Walker here again, have you decided what you're doing?"

"Oh yeah, I'll do the interview, no problem," said Shutty.

"Well, what we want you to do is to come to the training ground with a lunch box and some overalls."

"That's no problem, but I want five hundred quid for doing it and it's got to be cash."

"Okay, I'll sort that out."

Shutty turned up the next day at the training ground with his overalls and a lunch box. We got Steve Ellis, Wednesday's official photographer, to pretend to take some photos. I don't think there was even any film in his camera. Steve got him jumping up while holding his lunch box and a hammer and wearing these overalls. All the lads were watching from the pavilion, laughing their bollocks off.

There was one time when he broke his nose during a game and he said, "Strap it up and I'll go back out there!" Later, when we played together at Leeds, Shutty scored the winner against Stuttgart in the European Cup at the San Siro. The match, which I missed due to injury, was played there because a player who'd turned out in the original game was ineligible. After the game, Shutty was apparently stood in the corner of the dressing-room, trying to take in what had happened. All the lads were taking the piss out of him because he kept saying, "I can't believe it, I can't believe it, I've scored in the San Siro."

Mel STERLAND

Shutty was the tightest man in the world. If there were four of you in a car, he'd kneel down as if he was tying his laces when he got out, just so he didn't have to go to the bar first. The best thing was that he even did it when he was wearing slip-on shoes! I used to go to school with Shutty and we called him "Psycho" because he's a bit bonkers.

When we got to the semi-finals of the FA Cup that season, we were all sat there in the changing room, waiting for the draw to be made. When it came on the radio and the presenter said, "Sheffield Wednesday versus Everton" all the lads were saying, "Fucking hell, that's going to be tough," but Shutty punched the air and shouted, "Yes!"

"What are you on about?" we said to him.

"We've been drawn at home."

"Shutty, it's a semi-final so it's at a neutral ground."

"Oh yeah, I forgot."

Shutty ended up scoring in the game with a header, which was played at Villa Park but we lost 2-1. I was in tears afterwards because we should have beaten them. It was my second semi-final appearance after the game against Brighton three years earlier and I was on the losing side again, which was heartbreaking.

Me and Shutty scored both the goals when we won 2-0 at Manchester United in April 1986. We were unbeaten in the last seven games of the season and finished fifth. We'd have played in the UEFA Cup if it wasn't for the fact that English clubs were banned from playing in Europe at that time. We were gutted

Boozing, Betting & Brawling

because we'd worked hard that season to finish so high up the table.

A young defender called Ian Knight, who'd joined Wednesday after being released by Barnsley, was really starting to make an impression around that time. Sadly, his career was wrecked when he suffered a compound fracture following a challenge from Chester's Gary Bennett during an FA Cup fourth round replay at Hillsborough. I didn't play in the game, so I was sat in the stand when Knight's leg was broken. Above the crowd noise, you could hear the bone break; it was a sickening sound. "Knighty" was a very good player who'd got everything and I used to call him "Alan Hansen". I think he'd have played for England had it not been for that injury. Ian was left with one leg shorter than the other and I think he got about a million pounds in compensation. That's a lot of money, but I think he might have earned more if he'd been able to carry on playing. I later saw Gary Bennett in a bar in Spain during a pre-season trip when I had a go at him over that challenge. I went up and told him what I thought of him. "You've fucking ruined Ian Knight's career," I said, jabbing my finger in his direction. "You horrible bastard – you don't deserve to be a fucking player, doing that." He apologised for what he did, but I was having none of it. "You fucking twat, what did you think you were doing?" He was close to tears by the time I'd finished and left the bar sharpish.

On the same trip, I nearly ended up killing Charlie Williamson! We went out into the sea on a pedalo when we were still pissed after having some beers the night before. I was doing all the pedalling and he fell asleep, so I pushed him into the water. He took ages to come up and I was panicking like mad until he suddenly appeared. Charlie still brings that story up regularly. He says that he thought it was all over for him because he was fast asleep when I pushed him over the side of the boat. When he got back into the boat, we went back to shore and I bought him a San Migel, so he was happy.

A Scottish defender called Ken Brannigan, who was signed from Queens Park, made his debut at Leicester during the 1986/87 season. We got hammered 6-1 and Brannigan was shocking. In fact, I'd go as far as saying it was the worst debut I've ever seen. I wasn't able to play that day due to injury, so I went to a chippy near the ground before kick-off and ordered pie, chips and peas. I was walking along, eating my food, when this idiot came up to me and said, "Aren't you playing today, Mel?"

"Yeah, I'm just eating this and then going down for the second half," I replied sarcastically.

It was a windy day and the rain was pissing down when we faced Coventry at Hillsborough. The Coventry keeper, Steve Ogrizovic, was at the Leppings Lane end of the ground and he booted the ball up field. With the wind taking hold of the ball, I knew it would go straight to Martin Hodge, so I turned round to run up the wing, ready to help launch an attack, fully expecting that Hodgey would soon be making a clearance. As I looked forward, I saw the Coventry fans jumping up and down, celebrating. Then I turned to see Hodgey picking the ball out of the net. As I saw later on video, the ball had bounced over his head, which was a joke really. Hodgey then had a bit of a torrid time because after letting that one in, he let another sloppy goal in.

Boozing, Betting & Brawling

When we were playing Chelsea, David Speedie was being a pain in the arse, so at half-time our chief scout John Harris went over to Paul Hart and said, "The best thing you can do to him is blummin' elbow him on the blummin' head." Sure enough, in the second half, "Harty" jumped up, smacked Speedie on his head and that was him done. Harty was great with us, not the serious guy you saw when he was a manager at clubs like Nottingham Forest and Barnsley. If you looked at him when he was a manager, it was just like watching Howard Wilkinson.

The owner of Josephine's Nightclub, Dave Allen, who was later the chairman of Sheffield Wednesday, used to give a magnum of champagne to any player who scored a hat-trick. We played Stockport in the second round of the League Cup and after beating them 3-0 at home in the first-leg, we played the return match at Manchester City's Maine Road ground because of the number of fans we had. Colin Walker scored a hat-trick and I got two goals in a 7-0 rout. When me and Walker were on two goals apiece, I went through and all Walker had got to do was pull the ball back for me to score and complete my hat-trick. He decided to shoot instead and the ball went under the keeper and into the net. So having scored a hat-trick, off Walker went down to Josephine's – somewhere he never used to go – and just walked off with this magnum of champagne. That pissed me off so much because I was a regular in Josephine's.

David Hirst, someone who went on to become a legendary player at Hillsborough, joined Wednesday from Barnsley that season. "Hirsty" is a great lad and even now he calls me "Skip" because I was the captain when he arrived at the club. I remember when he made his debut, the rest of us were having omelette and beans or chicken and beans and Hirsty had bacon sandwiches! We were all sat down when these bacon sandwiches were brought over, enough for about four or five people, and Hirsty ate the lot. He found it difficult when he first came to the club before finding his form and doing a superb job for Wednesday.

Towards the end of the 1986/87 season, I came up against my good mate Imre Varadi, who was playing in midfield for Manchester City when they came to Hillsborough. I got the ball, cut inside him, then went on the outside and he brought me down in the area. The referee pointed to the spot straight away. It was a penalty, but Imre obviously didn't think it was. "You cheating fat bastard," he said to me as I got to my feet. I had a go back at him before Brian Marwood took the penalty and scored. As I ran past Imre, he again called me a "fat bastard", but we were both having a laugh about what had happened. City were doing well as the game went on, putting us under pressure and Imre managed to get into the box and score. He ran towards me after scoring, again told me I was a "fat bastard" and held up a finger from each hand to indicate that it was 1-1. At that moment, I just wanted to boot him all over the field! I had the last laugh when Lee Chapman scored the winner.

Veteran defender Steve McCall was signed from Ipswich in the summer of 1987. We called him "Dracula" because he used to take his front two teeth out. "Mr Grumpy" was another nick-name we had for him because he was a

Boozing, Betting & Brawling

miserable bastard!

Another player who signed for us in pre-season was David Armstrong, who arrived from Southampton, but he ended up only lasting three days. The official story put out was that he didn't want to take his kid out of school, but that was a load of bollocks. It was down to the fact that he didn't like Howard Wilkinson's physically demanding training sessions. He trained with us and as usual we were doing a lot of running. We then went on tour to Germany and Armstrong played in a game against Armenia Bielefeld. When Wilko held a training session, Armstrong clearly wasn't happy when all we did was run. "That's it, I'm off," he said, "I'm a footballer, not a fucking runner." With that he took off his tracksuit and headed back to the south coast. Armstrong lost his hair at a young age and Carl Bradshaw used to call him "Uncle Festa" after the character in the *Addams Family*.

We got off to a bad start that season and found ourselves third from bottom after a 3-0 defeat at home to Coventry. Among several players signed by Howard Wilkinson to strengthen the squad was Colin West, who arrived from Glasgow Rangers. Wednesday fans have never forgotten his penalty-miss in a game. It was a terrible effort and the ball ended up in Herries Road! After that he got slaughtered and I felt sorry for "Westy" because he was a good lad.

I had another scrap with Martin Hodge after the FA Cup third round tie at Everton when we conceded a goal in the last minute, making it 1-1 and meaning we had to have a replay. Hodgey had caught a cross from Trevor Steven and chucked the ball out to Nigel Worthington who tried to knock the ball over the full-back, but it got cut out and they scored from the resulting cross. After the game, Hodgey started having a go at Worthington in the dressing-room. I defended Worthington, telling Hodgey that he should take the blame. I said, "Hold on Hodgey, you shouldn't have fucking given it to him – you should have booted the ball up-field. It's your fucking fault we've drawn this." Hodgey got up and we both started firing punches at each other. He caught me with a beauty, to be honest, landing a good right hook, the bastard! But then we just got on with it. The goal we conceded at Goodison Park proved to be costly because when we went back to Hillsborough for the replay, we got hammered 5-0 with Graeme Sharp getting a hat-trick.

I scored a lot of goals for a defender, but one I scored against Arsenal in a 3-3 draw at Hillsborough at the end of that season stands out in my memory. I picked the ball up in the 18-yard box at the Kop end and went on a mazy run, going past Graham Rix, Liam Brady and Kenny Sansom, before getting into the 18-yard box at the Leppings Lane end and smashing the ball past John Lukic into the top corner of the net. Unfortunately, I've not got the goal on tape because it was in the third minute and the cameraman was slow in getting up to the gantry, so he didn't film it. It's a shame because it was a wonder goal and it would be nice to watch it again. Fans who were at the game still come up to me and talk about that goal.

A week after the Arsenal match, we were thrashed 5-1 by champions Liverpool in our final home game of the season. It was a disappointing campaign which turned out to be my last full season as a Wednesday player.

CHAPTER EIGHT

One-Cap Wonder

I was proud to represent England, first as an Under-21 international and then making the step-up to the full squad.

I helped the Under-21s win the European Championship in 1984, which featured some memorable matches. In the quarter-finals, we beat France 6-1 at Hillsborough and I scored with a drive at the Leppings Lane end after a free-kick was touched to me. After beating Italy in the semi-finals, we faced Spain in the final and I scored the only goal of the game in the first-leg in Seville after playing a one-two with Paul Bracewell. We completed a 3-0 win on aggregate in the return match at Bramall Lane following goals from Mark Hateley and Howard Gayle.

I enjoyed working with the England Under-21 coach Dave Sexton and he

Mel STERLAND

once described me as the best-ever right-back to have played for England at that level, which was some tribute.

England Under-21 caps arrived for both me and Gary Shelton at Sheffield Wednesday's training ground. They'd been packaged and sent through the post and we were messing about, putting the caps on our heads and showing them off to the rest of the players. Imre Varadi disappeared off to the toilets and came back with toilet paper wrapped round his head, like a turban. "You might have got your England caps," he said as he rejoined us, "but mine's better than yours. This is my India cap!" Everybody just fell about.

A year after helping the Under-21s win the European Championship, I was named in a couple of full squads, but I was forced to pull out both times due to injury. On one occasion, it was after Norwich winger Ruel Fox stamped on me during a game. When I first got into the full squad, we met up at a London hotel and I was shitting myself because all the big-hitters were there, playing for the likes of Manchester United and Liverpool. I was from Sheffield Wednesday and I was thinking, "What's happening here?" One player who helped me settle in straight away was Paul Gascoigne who'd been in a few squads and made you feel welcome. "Gazza" is a great guy and I've never known anyone like him. We were in the players' lounge at Wembley when he went over to my missus, who's got big boobs, saying, "Ooh, you're lovely. I can see why Mel always has a smile on his face, going home to whoppers like them!" Charmaine just looked at me and started laughing. Gazza didn't take time saying it – he just came straight out with it.

Boozing, Betting & Brawling

Gary Lineker got into the squad at the same time as me, but then he went big time, which was disappointing. I asked him to sign some autographs when he was just a squad player and he used to sign them. But when he got into the side, I asked him for an autograph and he just said, "I'm fucking fed up of signing autographs for you." That pissed me off, especially as it was for a mentally handicapped person in Rotherham. His attitude was a joke really and I wanted to chin him to be honest, but I couldn't really do that as a member of the England set-up, so I just booted him when Sheffield Wednesday played Tottenham, wellying him on the half-way line, which gave me a bit of satisfaction!

I won the first of two "B" caps in 1987, when we played in Malta. We won 2-0 and I scored a wonder goal from about 35 yards. Mick Harford scored one from about four yards – putting it in with his knob – and that goal was shown on TV instead of mine, which was a joke.

Howard Wilkinson spoke to the England management and pressed my claims for another senior call-up. "Mel's doing well for us and I think he deserves a chance," he said. It was Howard who told me I'd been selected to travel to Saudi Arabia for a friendly international in 1988. It was fantastic and I nearly dropped bow-legged when I heard the news, but then I sat down and thought, "I'm doing well for Sheffield Wednesday and I think I deserve to get picked". I was playing well, making goals and scoring them.

We flew out to Saudi Arabia on Concorde, which was a great experience, eating fillet steak on the flight. I roomed with Gary Pallister and I can remember asking him for some of his chocolate. But he was a tight bastard with his chocolate – he loved it and would never give you any.

Bobby Robson was the England manager at that time and he used to get players names mixed up. He once called Gazza "Rocastle" in training – mistaking him for Arsenal's black midfielder David Rocastle – and I just looked at him and thought, "Fucking hell, his eyes have gone". Bobby's a great bloke and he was still managing at the top level well into his seventies. I don't know how he did it.

It was the night before the match when I was told I was in the side, which was a fantastic feeling. After the team had been announced, a few of us played a joke on Paul Parker, who was a horrible little bastard. He was just a big-headed twat who loved himself. I was with Gazza, Chris Waddle and Dave Beasant in one of the hotel rooms when we decided to play a trick on Parker. Waddle told Parker he'd got to go down to the reception because Bobby Robson wanted to see him about playing, supposedly because I wasn't feeling well. So he went down to the reception and when he came back to his room, we were waiting with a bed-sheet. He opened the door and we chucked the bed-sheet over him. Waddle and Gazza were on him and I'd got this fork in my hand and went to stab the bed-sheet, but the fork slipped in my hand and went straight in his arse! So he's there with a fork stuck in his arse and me, Gazza, Wadds and Beasant were laughing our balls off. We'd done him good style. He was screaming and shouting, "You bastards, you've set me up, you bastards." It was so good because he'd gone down to the reception thinking he was going

I'm on the right in this early photo of me and my twin brother Glyn.

A photo I cherish of Mum and Dad.

With Dad and Glyn, who has a dummy in his mouth.

In the school team – I'm second from the left.

The Middlewood Rovers team. I'm third from the right on the back row. Frank Ashton is far left on the back row and Carl Shutt is next to him. On the far right is Albert Phelan. Charlie Williamson is on the front row, third from the right. Also on the front row (second from the left) is John Eastwood, who is a big Wednesdayite.

Sheffield Wednesday's youth team. I'm third from the right on the back row again. "Taffy" is second from the right with Peter Shirtliff third from the left. Players on the front row include Charlie Williamson (second from the left), Craig Howard (second from the right) and Kevin Taylor (far right).

An early photo of me in the Sheffield Wednesday first-team.

Celebrating a victory with, er, bottles of milk!

Receiving the keys to a sponsored car from a local dealership.

A familiar pose – scoring from the penalty spot.

With my wife Charmaine on our wedding day.

Scoring a penalty against Crystal Palace which secured promotion to the First Division in 1984.

Toasting our promotion success. Not a milk bottle in sight this time!

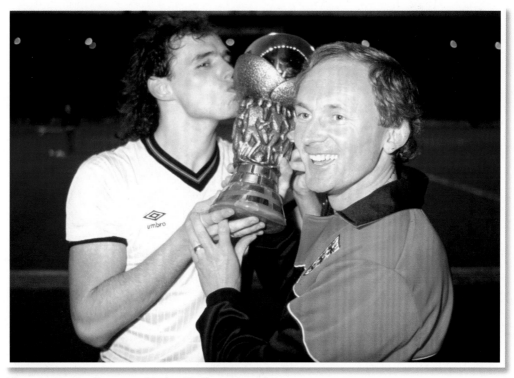

After winning the European Under-21 Championship.

Now they're what
you call shorts!

I was so proud to captain Sheffield Wednesday.
Here I am with my Nottingham Forest counterpart
Stuart Pearce.

Powering a header past Coventry City keeper Steve Ogrizovic.

On a fishing trip with the Wednesday squad.

The expectant parents shortly before the arrival of Chantelle Louise.

Joined by my sister-in-law Sarah at a fancy dress party.

In tears after the FA Cup semi-final defeat at the hands of Everton in 1986.

Dad holding one of my football trophies.

Charmaine's family join us at Nathan's christening. Next to me is my brother-in-law Christopher and his sister Sarah is holding Nathan. Charmaine's parents, Christine and Sammy, are in the middle and her other brother Anthony is on the far right, holding Chantelle.

On the attack against Manchester United with Gordon Strachan looking on. We later became team-mates at Leeds.

With the full England squad ahead of my one and only appearance against Saudi Arabia.

MANAGER: G. SOUNESS

SECRETARY: R.C. OGILVIE

——THE——
RANGERS
FOOTBALL CLUB plc
—Founded 1873—

FINANCIAL AGREEMENT - MELVYN STERLAND

The player's basic wage will be paid as follows:-

3rd March 1989	-	31st July 1990	£1,500 per week
1st August 1990	-	31st July 1991	£1,700 per week
1st August 1991	-	31st July 1992	£1,800 per week
1st August 1992	-	30th June 1993	£2,000 per week

Provided the above named is a Registered player with Rangers Football
Club upon each of the following dates, he shall be entitled to
receive additional remunerations as follows:-

3rd March 1989	-	£25,000
1st August 1990	-	£25,000
1st August 1991	-	£25,000
1st August 1992	-	£25,000

Date ...3.3.89...   Signed ....
RANGERS F.C.

Date ...3.3.89.....   Signed ....
MELVYN STERLAND

Witness ....

Witness ....

REGISTERED OFFICE: IBROX STADIUM GLASGOW G51 2XD TEL: 041-427 5232 TELEX: 779565 FAX: 041-42
Registered in Scotland No. 4276

The terms of the contract I signed at
Glasgow Rangers.

As my appearance in a kilt shows, we soon adjusted
to life in Scotland. My spell at Rangers was
unfortunately all too brief.

With our friends Charlie & Louise Williamson
and Tom & Sandra Graham at Ibrox.

We're photographed before attending
a function.

The start of nine in a row. Celebrating winning the
Scottish Premier League title with my Rangers
team-mates.

Fit and raring to go as a
Leeds United player.

In action for Leeds against West Yorkshire neighbours Bradford City.

'King Cracker' with me, Charmaine and our friends Andy and Audrey Hobson.

With my brothers and sisters. At either side of me at the front are Sheila and Sharon. Middle row – Malcolm, John and Glyn. Back row – Terry and George. Avril passed away before this photo was taken.

Scoring a crucial penalty against Manchester United on the way to winning the title.

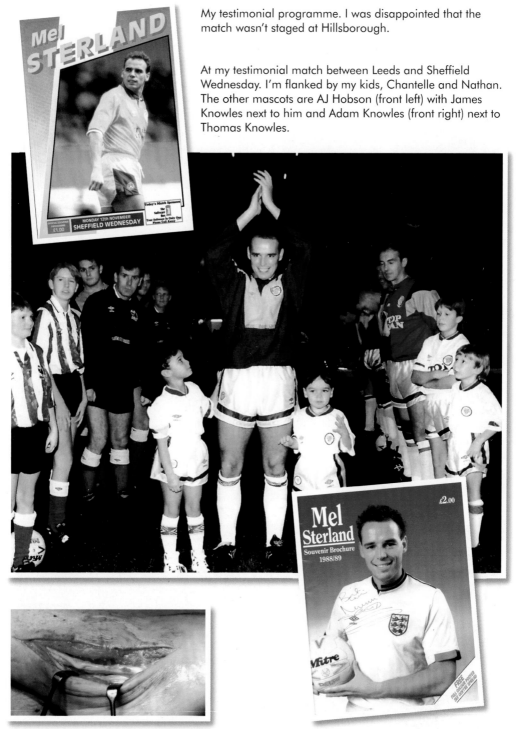

My testimonial programme. I was disappointed that the match wasn't staged at Hillsborough.

At my testimonial match between Leeds and Sheffield Wednesday. I'm flanked by my kids, Chantelle and Nathan. The other mascots are AJ Hobson (front left) with James Knowles next to him and Adam Knowles (front right) next to Thomas Knowles.

Not for the faint-hearted! My right ankle was operated on a number of times before I was forced to call it a day.

The programme for my second testimonial match, which was arranged when I was manager of Boston United.

Re-united with my old Leeds team-mates and manager Howard Wilkinson at the opening of 'Howard's Bar' at Elland Road.

We were lucky enough to meet Mick Hucknall when he performed with Simply Red at Sheffield Arena.

Three generations of the Sterland family. Pictured with our children Nathan and Chantelle, along with grandson Leon.

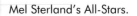

Mel Sterland's All-Stars.

to play instead of me and there was no way he was going to. And we just thought it was so funny that I'd stabbed him in the arse because we didn't get on with him. He was a "big-time Charlie" who used to strut around but he got his comeuppance that day.

We played in the national stadium in Kuwait, which was an incredible place. There were solid gold toilet chains and the taps were also gold. When they played the national anthem before kick-off, it made the hairs on the back of my neck stand up.

The date was 16 November 1988 and I took my place in the following line-up:

David Seaman, Mel Sterland, Stuart Pearce, Gary Pallister, Tony Adams, Michael Thomas, Bryan Robson, David Rocastle, Chris Waddle, Peter Beardsley, Gary Lineker

We drew 1-1 and it was a crap game. We were winning 1-0 when they got a corner and I was shouting at Michael Thomas to get in front. I went to close down the player who was threatening, slipped and the guy went through and scored. Nobody played well, but because I slipped for the goal, I felt I got all the blame. Bobby Robson got slated in the tabloids after the game. One of the headlines was: "IN THE NAME OF ALLAH, GO".

I got in one or two squads after that, but again I got injured and my international career was effectively over. I did actually make one further international appearance when I appeared as a substitute in a "B" team game against Yugoslavia in December 1989. I was disappointed that I didn't win any more caps, especially as the regular choice at right-back, Gary Stevens, was my understudy for the England Under-21s. He couldn't get in the side when I was fit but when I got injured he took my place and then went on to win 46 full caps.

I believe that if you're playing well for your club, you should get selected for your country. It didn't work like that though because players who got selected for their country got selected again, regardless of how they were performing at club level. Everton were doing well at that time so that probably gave Gary Stevens the edge over me. Gary was a very defensive-minded player who rarely got forward. I was a different type of player because with Sheffield Wednesday and Leeds playing five at the back, it meant I got forward as much as I could.

Who knows, if Michael Thomas had been listening to me in that Saudi Arabia match, we'd have won and I'd probably have got more caps. But it wasn't to be and I had to settle for the one.

CHAPTER NINE

Time To Move On

As the captain of Sheffield Wednesday, I often represented the club at presentation nights. On one occasion I agreed to do a presentation at Middlewood Hospital in Sheffield, where they treated people with mental problems. After doing the presentation, they presented me and Charmaine with a rocking horse that the patients had made for Chantelle. One of the female patients then asked me for a dance while Charmaine chatted with one of the members of staff. "How long has she been here?" Charmaine asked the nurse.

"She's been here most of her life," the nurse replied.

"Why, what did she do?"

"She's an arsonist; she just sets fire to people. You've got to keep your eye on her because your back can be turned and she'll set your jacket on fire."

Mel STERLAND

I was dancing away with this woman and it was obvious she wasn't a full shilling, but I was totally oblivious to just how dangerous she was.

I'd made plans to buy a sports shop in the Darnall area of Sheffield and it was all set to go through until Howard Wilkinson advised me against it. It was my testimonial year and Howard said that I'd got to concentrate on football. "When people come to the shop, they'll want to see you," he said. "You've got that much on at the moment, so you won't be able to spend time there. If you buy that sports shop, you'll not be in Wednesday's plans."

Charmaine was as keen to buy the shop as I was, but we had no choice other than to pull out of the deal. However, the guy who was selling the shop didn't appreciate the position we were in and he's always held the breakdown of the sale against us. It turned out to be good advice from Howard because it wasn't long before the shop closed.

We had a problem at the ground for a while when a smartly dressed bloke used to turn up, saying that he was there to see the manager. He looked the part, wearing a suit and tie and carrying a briefcase, so nobody questioned him. It later turned out that he was trying to get into the changing room to nick any cash, credit cards and expensive watches he could lay his hands on. He was doing the same at other local clubs such as Sheffield United, Barnsley, Rotherham and Chesterfield. Word got around about what he was doing, but not before he'd raided our changing room and relieved me of a large wad of cash I'd received from sales of my testimonial brochure. The brochures sold really well in the club shop and I used to go there to collect the money I was

Boozing, Betting & Brawling

owed. This particular day I collected about £600 in cash before I went to the changing room. When I got changed and went out to train, I left the cash with my clothes, thinking that it would be safe there. But when I got back into the dressing room, I found that the money had gone. I was gutted because six hundred quid was quite a lot of money to me. I should have left it in the shop, but it's easy to say that with hindsight.

I can still picture the guy who took my money; he was only a little bloke with black hair. I wish I could see him now! He was eventually rumbled when Alan Smith asked him who he wanted to see. When he told him that he was there to see the manager, Alan told him to wait for a moment. I think Alan had an inkling about what the guy was doing so he got someone to phone the police. When the guy said that he wanted to go outside to take a look at the pitch, Alan insisted on going with him so that he didn't run off. When the police arrived and searched him, they found that he'd got a briefcase full of money, credit cards and watches. Then they took him outside to his car and saw that his boot was also full of stuff he'd nicked, apart from my six hundred quid! I didn't get anything back because he'd obviously spent it.

There was another bloke who used to come to the training ground, collecting autographs. We thought he'd come from the local mental hospital, because he seemed to be a nutter, but he must have just been acting daft because he nicked all our money as well! We all gave him autographs then went out training and came back to find our wallets missing. With the money players earn nowadays, it'd be frightening to think of what a thief could leg off with if they broke into a

Mel STERLAND

Premiership club's training ground. Mind you, I think it would be hard to get in because of all the security they have in place. In our day, there were no stewards on the gate so people just used to stroll in. Fans could come into the training ground and watch us train, which was good.

There was a major upheaval at Hillsborough early in the 1988/89 season when Howard Wilkinson resigned to take over at Leeds. I was obviously disappointed when Howard left because he'd had such an influence on me, but I could understand his reasons for going. He felt that he'd taken Wednesday as far as he could at that time and perhaps Leeds had more ambition. Howard asked his assistant, Peter Eustace, to go with him to Elland Road, but Eustace decided to stay at Hillsborough. He was named caretaker-manager and then landed the job on a permanent basis after we won at Southampton at the end of October to go fifth.

I had a spell up front when all the forwards were injured at the start of the season. After playing as a centre-forward when I was a kid, it wasn't new to me so I had no fears about playing there. I scored on the opening day at home to Luton and scored again in the following game at Nottingham Forest, getting on the end of a corner with a header. Things were going well, but then Eustace took the captaincy off me, so I went to see him.

"What are you doing, taking the captaincy off me?" I asked.

"Well, I want somebody who's playing at the back, so they can see what's happening in the game," he replied.

I asked him to switch me back to right-back, but he refused and gave the

Boozing, Betting & Brawling

captaincy to Nigel Pearson. That killed me because after supporting Wednesday as a kid, captaining the team was tremendous and I didn't want to give up the role. It hurt that I'd had it taken off me through no fault of my own, after helping out the team by playing up front. After going back to right-back when the strikers were fit, I never got the captaincy back, which left me feeling absolutely gutted. I thought Eustace was wrong to do that and I never forgave him. We had an argument and I asked for a move. After arguing with Peter at the training ground, I tried to leave, but someone had locked the door from the outside, so I finished up punching the door. A day or so later, Eustace got the push.

Eustace used to be known as the "Squire of Stocksbridge" because a lot of people thought he was arrogant. There's no doubt that he was arrogant – and apparently he was also like that as a player – but I didn't really have any problems with him apart from the time when he took the captaincy off me. I felt sorry for him, to be honest, because he had a hard time when he took over from Wilko. Eustace was fantastic as the caretaker-manager and the players got him the job with some good results, but he seemed to change all of a sudden after landing the role on a full-time basis. Things just didn't go well for him and we had a terrible run which resulted in him being sacked.

Wednesday appointed Ron Atkinson as manager after sacking Eustace. During Ron's first training session, we were all in the middle of the pitch at the training ground on a windy day and what was left of Big Ron's hair just lifted up, but nobody dared laugh because he'd just taken over. Ron soon identified what was missing from our side and signed three black players – Carlton Palmer,

Mel STERLAND

Dalian Atkinson and Mark Taylor – within weeks. A lot was made of some comments Ron made about Marcel Desailly a few years ago when a microphone was left switched on following a TV commentary. He'll have been disappointed with what he said and he's apologised for his comments, but I don't think for one minute that Ron is racist. The fact that he positively encouraged the inclusion of black players in the team proved that.

Glasgow Rangers boss Graeme Souness was alerted to the fact that I'd asked for a transfer and he invited me to Glasgow for talks. I went with Charmaine and we headed to Ibrox where we were given a tour of the stadium and taken to the trophy room, which was full of silverware. A security guard took us round the stadium and neither of us could understand a word he was saying because of his broad Scottish accent. I just kept saying "pardon" to him and my missus also kept asking him to repeat himself, so he must have thought we were both bleedin' deaf!

After that, we were taken to meet Souness, who took us to his home in Edinburgh. The house was absolutely magnificent, with a large, galleried staircase. We were due to stay the night there, but that plan was soon scuppered. After putting our suitcases in one of the guest bedrooms, the phone rang and it was Ron Atkinson, telling Souness that he wanted us to go back to Sheffield.

When we got back to Sheffield, I went to see Ron, who was staying at the Hallam Towers hotel. I walked into his suite and found him sat there, drinking champagne. Ron said that he didn't want to lose me, but I told him that I'd

Boozing, Betting & Brawling

made my mind up that I wanted to go. I explained that I'd served Wednesday for 11 years and thought the time was right to move on. But Ron didn't want me to go straight away because it would have looked bad for him, so he tried to persuade me to stay. "If I don't do this, it's going to look like I've moved here and flushed you out and that's not what I want the fans to think," he said. "That's why I've had to call you back." When I asked him if my move to Rangers was going ahead, he said, "I'm not saying it's impossible, but there are a few things we've got to sort out." After I had the conversation with Ron, he looked down at my feet and saw I'd got no socks on. "The next time you come and see me, make sure you've got some socks on," he said before starting to laugh. I looked at his feet and saw he'd got no socks on either!

I was adamant that I wanted to go to Rangers and when I spoke to Wednesday coach Frank Barlow, he told me it would be a great move for me and urged me to give it a go. I thought that was fantastic, coming from someone who was at the club. There was a story in the local 'paper saying that I could be staying at Hillsborough, but Wednesday agreed a fee with Rangers later that week and I flew up to Glasgow with Charmaine to sort everything out.

Talks went very well – although I didn't need much persuading – and agreed a deal worth fifteen hundred quid a week, plus bonuses. I'd only been on four hundred quid at Wednesday, so it was a massive jump in salary. Everyone thought I was on big money at Wednesday because I was one of the top players there. But you tended to find that when you played for your local side after coming through the ranks, they didn't give a toss about you. They only really looked after the players they'd signed and the local lads got crapped on. I don't know if that happens as much now, but it did then.

After agreeing personal terms, I had a medical and signed a four-year contract. Although it was a massive step to leave a club that I'd supported as a boy, which did hurt, it was a fresh start for me and my family and I couldn't wait to play for Rangers.

CHAPTER TEN

Four Months In Glasgow

A lot of people thought I moved to Rangers for the money, but that wasn't the case. In fact, with the way things turned out, I ended up losing a lot of money up there. The fact was that I wanted to play in Europe, although that unfortunately didn't happen.

We initially stayed in a cottage at the back of a hotel, run by a couple called Tom and Sandra. My mother-in-law and her sister used to come up to stay at the hotel and Tom used to spoil them because he was the chef. He'd cook them the best food and Rangers paid for it all. Rangers were fantastic when it came to helping you settle in because they really looked after you. The chairman, Mr Holmes, even used to drive Charmaine around, looking for a house.

Things didn't get off to a good start for me at Rangers because I dropped a bollock on my first day at the club. As well as being clean-shaved, you had to wear a collar and tie when you reported for training and I went in wearing a green tie. Green is of course the colour associated with Celtic, so that went down well! All the lads stared at me when I walked in and it was only then that I realised what I'd done. Davie Cooper was a mad keen Rangers fan and he marked my card about the extent of the rivalry between Rangers and Celtic. "Mel, I just want to give you some advice," he said. "Don't wear that fucking green tie again." Davie, who referred to Celtic fans as "Fenian bastards", was laughing, but I knew that it was good advice and I never wore green again when I was on duty for Rangers.

The religious stuff was all new to me – I thought I'd just gone up there to play football. It was like the time when Gazza started messing about in an Old Firm game, pretending to play a flute. You listen to all these songs like "Fuck the Pope and the IRA" and think, "What's going on here"?

The Rangers fans were absolutely fantastic and gave me a great reception when I made my debut against Hamilton Accies. The game was played at a hundred miles an hour. I thought it would slow down, but it didn't and I couldn't get my breath. I thought, "I hope it isn't like this all the way through the season". But I managed to get through it okay and to cap a memorable day, I scored, which was fantastic. I can remember it as though it was yesterday. I went over to the fans to celebrate, thinking they were Rangers fans, but I dropped a bollock because they were Hamilton supporters!

The dressing-room was fantastic, with a lot of English players at the club,

Boozing, Betting & Brawling

which made it easy for me to settle in. As well as Butcher, Wilkins and Woods, there was Kevin Drinkell, Mark Walters and Gary Stevens. There was no split at all between the English and Scottish players at Ibrox. Among the Scottish players was Ally McCoist, who was a fruit and nut case, singing all the time. I used to room with another Scot, Davie Cooper, who sadly died prematurely. We also used to go to the betting shop together. He was a great guy and a superb footballer who's obviously very much missed in Scotland.

The fans were great with me as well and they used to sing, "Mel, Mel, Super Mel, Super Mel Sterland" and "Zico" came into it as well. We were on about £500 for a win and we hardly lost.

One thing that I was disappointed about was my position in the team. I thought I'd be playing as a wing-back, like I did at Sheffield Wednesday, but it didn't work out that way. When I first spoke to him, Graeme Souness said he was going to play Gary Stevens as a sweeper with Terry Butcher, Richard Gough, me and another player in the defensive roles. But that didn't happen because I was used as a right-winger instead. I hated playing in that position because I was never a right-winger in a million years, but we were winning so I just kept my mouth shut and got on with it.

When we played St Johnstone in the semi-finals of the Scottish Cup at Celtic Park, I was a substitute. It was an unremarkable 0-0 draw but the game stands out in my memory because it was the day of the Hillsborough Disaster. I heard people talking about the events at Hillsborough and I could hardly take in what they were saying. Some of my friends were at Hillsborough that day and obviously I was worried about them. I eventually found out they were all safe and well but it was devastating to hear how many people had died.

We played Celtic in the Scottish Cup Final and I can remember kicking Paul McStay and the late Tommy Burns, who were both very good players. I was substituted and replaced by Graeme Souness and we lost 1-0 following a defensive mistake. Gary Stevens tried to lay the ball back to Chris Woods, but Joe Miller nipped in and turned the ball into the empty net. I was gutted because I'd got a bonus of seven grand written into my contract for winning the Scottish Cup. I don't know what bonus the other players would have won, but I'd imagine it would have been a lot more than that because most of them had played in all the rounds leading up to the final, whereas I hadn't.

It was a great day, but it all went so quickly. After the game, I was picked out along with Kevin Drinkell for drug testing. It was all new to me but apparently they pick your number out of a hat. We had to provide a urine sample for testing and it took us ages to produce. We were drinking can after can of lager and I think we had about eight or nine cans apiece before we could piss. So not only did we have our piss tested but we got pissed as well!

I had a feeling I wouldn't be there the following season. Souness went mad in the dressing room, picking up his medal and chucking it against the wall. He raged, "You fucking bunch of bastards, you fucking cunts, letting those bastards beat you." All the players were looking round, trying not to catch his eye, when he added, "Right, fucking read the 'papers in the summer." He then went and signed Mo Johnston – which I presume was what he was referring to – but I'd

Boozing, Betting & Brawling

been sold by then.

You can look at the all the big derby games in England – Liverpool v Everton, Manchester United v Manchester City and Sheffield Wednesday v Sheffield United – and none of them compare to a Glasgow derby. That's bigger than any of them by far. The noise from the crowd is incredible during Old Firm matches. It's so loud that you can't hear when one of your team-mates is shouting something to you.

I never had a problem with Celtic fans when I went out socially because you knew where you could go. My old Sheffield Wednesday team-mate Chris Morris was at Celtic and we used to invite him and his wife round to our hotel, but we were told that wasn't a good idea so I thought it was best if we kept our distance. It just wasn't worth stirring anything up.

We made up for the disappointment of losing in the Scottish Cup Final by winning the Premier League and I scored twice against Hearts in the game that saw us seal the title. My first goal came when Mark Walters crossed from the left and I headed into the top corner. For my second, Ray Wilkins just tapped the ball to me and I bent it round the defensive wall. I followed that with an "aeroplane" celebration – holding my arms aloft – and even now the fans do that to me when I go up there, which is great. I should have scored three when I was in a good position, but Kevin Drinkell wouldn't pass to me, the greedy bastard! He ended up having a shot and scoring himself, denying me a hat-trick. Rangers dominated Scottish football at that time and it was their ninth title in a row.

Mel STERLAND

Everything had gone well in my first season at the club and I was happy with life in Scotland. We were about to buy a house at the Bridge of Allan, from one of Terry Butcher's mates, when I learned that I was being linked with a move in the English newspapers. We'd still got our house in Sheffield, but we were a week away from exchanging contracts, so I decided to go and find out from Graeme Souness what was happening. "Down in the south, it's in the 'papers that I'm for sale," I told him.

"I'm surprised at you Mel," he replied, "do you believe everything you read in the 'papers?"

"No, I don't, but I'm about to buy a house up here and I don't want to do that if I'm going to be moving."

"Look, go ahead and buy your house. Don't worry about it."

With that reassurance, we sold our house in Sheffield and moved into our new house in the Bridge of Allan, which is a nice area, with my team-mates Terry Butcher, Ray Wilkins and Chris Woods all living nearby. It was a lovely big detached house, with a snooker room and fields at the back with cows coming up to the fence. It was a bit different from the Manor estate where I grew up, with nine of us sharing a three-bedroom house! Chantelle started going to a little school at the bottom of the road and we were settling in.

After the season finished, we went down to Sheffield for a few days because Charmaine's mum was poorly. On the Thursday, the day we got back from Sheffield, the phone rang. Charmaine answered it and told me it was Ron Atkinson. "Fuck off, Ron Atkinson," I said. But she insisted it was, so I picked up the phone and asked who it was. The person at the other end replied, "It's Ron Atkinson."

"Fuck off, who's messing about?"

"It's Ron Atkinson at Sheffield Wednesday."

I was losing my patience by this point. "Come on, stop messing about, tell me who it is or I'll put the fucking phone down," I said.

"Mel, it's Ron Atkinson."

Finally realising it was him, I said, "Oh, sorry Ron, what can I do for you?"

"Do you want to come back to Sheffield Wednesday?" he replied.

I was a bit taken aback. "What do you mean?" I said, "I've signed a four-year contract up here, I've got a nice house and I'm happy."

"Well, let me just tell you something, you're for sale and I'd like to bring you back to Hillsborough. We'll look after you and give you a sponsored car."

He was only offering the same wages I was on before and I told him again that I wasn't interested, adding that I couldn't be for sale because I'd been assured by Graeme Souness that I was going nowhere. Ron's response suggested my future at Ibrox was not as secure as I thought. "Well, I think you'll find out that you'll be on your way," he said. I didn't really say anything else because I didn't know what to make of what he was saying and the conversation ended.

As soon as I put the phone down on Big Ron, Queens Park Rangers manager Trevor Francis rang me up and asked if I was interested in going to Loftus Road. "Look," I replied, "I've had Big Ron on the phone, but I'm happy at Rangers."

Mel STERLAND

Francis wasn't put off, however, asking me if I wanted to go down to London for a chat. I again told him that I wasn't looking to move. Shortly afterwards, Leeds United director Bill Fotherby was on the phone, asking me if I wanted to discuss a move to Elland Road. Clearly something wasn't right and when I finished talking to Fotherby, Charmaine said, "You better phone Graeme Souness because they're not all ringing for nothing."

When I managed to get hold of Souness, who was in an Italian restaurant, I wasn't prepared for what he told me. "Look son, I'm going to let you go because I'm looking to bring Trevor Steven back," he said. "I've spent too much money and you're the only player I can get my money back on pretty quickly."

"Does that mean I can talk to anybody I want to?" I replied.

"Yes and I wish you luck, wherever you go to."

When I asked him if that was it, he told me that it was, adding, "We'll hopefully get back the money we paid for you."

We went away a few days after that, on the Sunday, but it wasn't the sort of enjoyable break we'd planned. With all the uncertainty surrounding my future, the holiday was ruined. I was gutted because I'd only been at Rangers four months and had started to put down roots. Souness had told me to go and buy a house, which I did. I'd also got my kids in private school and all of a sudden, I felt as though I'd been kicked in the bollocks. I didn't want to leave Rangers, but Souness went back on his word, which I thought was bad.

There was no doubt that after being told that I was surplus to requirements at Ibrox, I just had to get away. It was no good trying to dig my heels in because

Boozing, Betting & Brawling

if I'd stayed, Souness would have probably played me in the reserves for the rest of the three years on my contract. He would have made it hard, that's for sure. I know Graham Roberts had a massive fall-out with him and Souness used to send him with the kids or the reserves right up to the Highlands and never played him in the first-team.

Souness was difficult to get to know because he hardly used to speak to you. He used to play in all the games in training because he was a fit guy who loved tackling and getting in among people, winding them up. Walter Smith, who was a great guy, did all the coaching while Phil Boersma used to sort out the warm-ups. Souness takes Boersma with him everywhere he goes and they must have been big buddies at Liverpool.

Going to Rangers was a great move for me because we made a lot of friends in Scotland and still keep in touch with Tom and Sandra. Our family used to enjoy coming up to see us as well because it was such a nice place. I just wish I could have stayed there for the full four years on my contract because the Rangers fans didn't see me at my best, due to playing out of position.

I've been told that some Rangers supporters think I criticised the club when I left, but that simply isn't true. When we were doing some research for this book, one Rangers fan even posted on a message board saying that I'd described playing in an Old Firm match as "nothing special". I can only think that I was mis-quoted in the Scottish Press because I can honestly say that I've got nothing but good words to say about the club and the supporters.

Within four weeks of the removal men moving us into the house at the Bridge of Allan, they moved everything out and we lost money on the place. I also lost out when it came to my contract at Rangers. I had an agent called Jerome Anderson and I don't really think he did well for me. I never asked for a transfer from Rangers, so I thought he should have got me my signing-on fee, but I didn't get it. It was about a hundred grand, spread over four years, although I've been told that you're not entitled to the full amount if you've been at a club for less than a year. I received a quarter of the figure – twenty five grand – and we also lost about the same amount on the house up there.

After returning from Spain, I went down to QPR for talks with Trevor Francis, even though I didn't fancy the prospect of moving to London. As I was on my way to see Trevor, Howard Wilkinson phoned me. "Don't sign for QPR," he said. "On your way back up, come and talk to us. I'm going to sign some good players and win promotion with Leeds United."

When I went to QPR, they offered me a three-year contract, but it wasn't for me, so I decided to give it a miss. On the way home, as planned, I stopped off at a hotel in Nottingham and met Howard Wilkinson and his chief scout, Ian McParland. They sold the club to me and I had no hesitation in signing for Leeds. Howard said, "We'll win this league this year" and I was excited about the prospect of playing in a successful side.

CHAPTER ELEVEN

Re-United With Wilko

I was happy with the deal I agreed with Leeds. I was on two grand a week, with another grand in appearance money, which was good money. Leeds also agreed to pay for flights to Scotland because we still had our house to sell there.

Howard Wilkinson knew what I was all about of course after working with me at Sheffield Wednesday. He also knew which players would gel together and he'd already got the likes of Gordon Strachan, Chris Fairclough and Chris Whyte. Vinnie Jones had also just signed for the club. Everybody talks about Vinnie's hard man image, but I couldn't believe how fit he was and I think his fitness left Wilko gobsmacked. Press-ups and sit-ups were so easy for him – he was just naturally fit. Vinnie was a diamond kid who did ever so well for Leeds. Wilko knew what he was doing when he signed him because he got a player who he knew the crowd would love and they did.

I made my debut for Leeds on the opening day of the 1989/90 season when we went up to Newcastle. We were winning 2-0 and then got hammered 5-2 with Micky Quinn marking his debut for Newcastle with four goals. I can remember the return game clearly because I cracked a rib after clashing with Kevin Brock. I was in a lot of pain, but I carried on even though it hurt so much that I had to hold my ribs as I was running down the wing. Gordon Strachan knocked the ball over the full-back and I ran after it, controlled it and sent over a cross which was headed in by Ian Baird. It had been a tight game, but that goal saw us win 1-0. After the game I had to stay in hospital overnight. Not many teams liked to come to Leeds that season because the fans really got behind us and we had a full house every week.

Vinnie Jones loved to wind-up opposition players. We were 3-1 at Portsmouth and Vinnie had been having a bit of a tussle with Martin Kuhl, who was a horrible bastard. Making sure that Kuhl was within ear-shot, Vinnie turned to me and said, "Mel, this is fucking easy, this game. That'll be another five hundred quid win bonus." Vinnie then pretended to smoke a cigar to rub it in that we were coasting. After it went to 3-2, Mervyn Day threw the ball out to me. I got it under control and knocked it back to him but he was too slow to react, allowing Guy Whittingham to nip in, take the ball round him and make it 3-3. Kuhl came over to me and Vinnie and said, "You're getting no fucking win bonus now, are you?" It killed us in one, to be honest.

Vinnie was on a goals bonus and I remember him talking about what he was going to spend it on after scoring in one game. 'That's a grand so I've got my new bathroom suite,' he said. There were some others on goals bonuses and that's why they never passed the ball, the greedy bastards!

Another character who joined Leeds that season was Mickey Thomas. He was good to have in the dressing room because he used to come in and tell us some great stories. Mickey claimed that he'd been out on a boat, fishing with some mates, when he dropped his wallet overboard with his car keys and everything in it. He said, "We came back to shore and I went back about two hours later, walking on the beach, and there it was, my wallet with the keys in." We said, "Fuck off Mickey, you lying bastard." But he swore that it was true.

When Mickey was at Chelsea, he used to sleep in the grounds-man's hut on the night before a game. He's hyperactive and is on the go all the time. In fact, he's barking mad, but what a great kid and a fantastic footballer. Added to that, he was so fit that he could run all day. Mickey never used to have a proper shower. After training, he'd just go under the shower for a moment, get dried and changed and then get in his VW Golf and drive back to Wales.

All the players got on well together at Leeds and we had some good laughs. We were on tour in Ireland and as footballers, birds used to come on to you. We went back to the hotel and there were about four or five players there with one bird. She obviously wanted to go with the big-hitters in the team and we knew which room they were going in, so we went into the room ahead of them. I was with Micky Whitlow and Simon Grayson and we hid behind the curtains in the room. These two well-known players came back with this bird. They were

Mel STERLAND

on the bed and nothing was happening, they were only talking and drinking. Then they were having a kiss and a cuddle and Micky caught the curtain, so the bird shouts, "There's somebody behind that curtain." Micky and Simon looked at me and I shook my head as if to say, "I'm stopping here, so you better just walk out from behind this curtain." That's what Micky did, leaving me and Simon still there. It was a relief because Mick had got the smelliest breath in the world and we were face-to-face. Fair play to him though, because he owned up and walked out. So I'm there with "Larry" Grayson and again they're messing about on the bed. I'm trying to look through the curtains and my foot slipped off a little ledge. Again, she jumps and says, "There's somebody else behind that curtain." I whispered to Grayson, "You're going, I'm stopping" and off he went, leaving just me there. I was peeking at the three of them on the bed, but with me being like an elephant, my foot slipped again. This time, the bird gets up, pulls the curtains back and I'm there pretending to be a window cleaner. That sort of thing used to happen on tour. Players used to take birds back to the hotel and others would hide in wardrobes and watch them shagging.

On another tour, when we went to Spain, I ended up in a fight with Bobby Davison. At the airport, all the lads put in a fiver apiece to buy a ghetto blaster so we could listen to some music on the beach. At the end of the week, during one big drinking session, we were all pissed up, drinking tequila slammers and everything. I remember Gary Speed knocking back one of these slammers and then puking his guts up. We were having a great laugh. Jim Beglin, who's now doing co-commentary on ITV, lost his sunglasses. I could hear him with his Irish accent shouting, "Where's my fucking sunglasses?" He came over to me and asked me where they were, so I said, "I don't fucking know, I haven't got a clue." But he was still going on and on about these sunglasses and Lee Chapman stuck his nose in, saying I'd chucked them in the sea. But I'd chucked nothing in the sea and they were apparently under a table. I was pissed off with Chapman, so I said to him, "Shut up you big lanky bastard, mind your own business." We're having a go at each other and then Davison joins in. Chapman walked off, leaving me and Bobby having an argument over these sunglasses. I finally told Bobby to shut up and he said, "Come and make me shut up." Chris Fairclough grabbed hold of me and wouldn't let me go, but Imre Varadi said to Chris, "Let him go, fucking let him go," because he obviously wanted to see a fight. As I went over to hit Bobby, I slipped and fell to the floor. Bobby went to boot me in the head and I blocked him, then got up and whacked him straight in the gob. We went out the next day and everything was fine between us because that was the way it was.

We were at the hotel ready to go out, waiting for Vinnie Jones. Nobody knew where he was and we were all sat out on a wall in front of the hotel. The next thing we knew, a cop car came round the corner and when it pulled up, out stepped Vinnie. They'd arrested him for kicking a ball which apparently hit a woman who was having a drink on the beach. We had to wait for him to get ready and he nearly got in trouble again that night when we bumped into about eight rugby players in this bar in Magaluf. Vinny wanted to fight everybody but he's a great kid.

Mel STERLAND

Gordon Strachan always believed in developing a good team-spirit, so he used to organise meals out for players and wives. Gordon arranged for us to meet Rod Stewart on one occasion. They're good friends and he told us that all the players and wives would go to the NEC in Birmingham to see Rod in concert and then have a private party afterwards. We watched the concert and were then taken to a function room for the after-show party. Rod had only recently met Rachel Hunter at that time and he was with her when he joined us. It was quiet when they walked into the room because I think we were all in awe of Rod, so he said, "Well my God, I thought this was a party, not a wake." That broke the ice and by the end of the night Charmaine was singing the Doris Day song, *Black Hills of Dakota*, while she had her arms round him. He was so down-to-earth and friendly. Another pop star we met was Simply Red singer Mick Hucknall. Chris Waddle and him are big buddies and Wadds arranged for us to meet him after a concert at Sheffield Arena.

David Batty was a one-off. I've never known a player like him for not warming up. Instead of stretching, like you're supposed to do, he just used to go on the training pitch and boot balls all over the place. I don't know how he did it, but he never pulled a hamstring or a groin. When we were playing at Wolves, "Batts" ran past me and went straight up the players' tunnel while the game was still in full flow, leaving everybody wondering what was happening. When Batts emerged a few minutes later, ready to re-join the action, Wilko asked him what was wrong. "I had to go for a shit," he explained.

I had a chance to play against Sheffield United for the first time in my career

Boozing, Betting & Brawling

that season. I never faced them when I was at Sheffield Wednesday because the two clubs were never in the same division when I was in the side. I played in a testimonial game for United player Tony Kenworthy, but that was it. It was a different matter with Leeds because I came up against them a number of times and always seemed to score, which was good. I got a hell of a lot of stick from Unitedites because of that.

We were preparing to face United at Bramall Lane on Boxing Day and the week before the game I was in my local pub, having a bit of banter with some Blades fans I knew. One of them came over to me and said, "You won't score against us." I told him that I would and bet him a fiver on it. After the bet was struck, I asked him where he went in the ground. During the game we were awarded a free-kick and I went over to Gordon Strachan and said, "I'm going to hit this." Gordon said, "Nae, big man, you'll not score from here." But I wasn't going to be put off. "Just leave it, Gordon," I insisted. As soon as I hit it, I knew it was going in. The ball rose into the top corner of the goal and Blades keeper Simon Tracey didn't have a prayer. I then ran over to the right-hand corner towards where the lad I'd had a bet with was and I was dancing round the corner flag. I wasn't taking the piss out of United, I was taking the piss out of this mate of mine. He still hasn't paid me the fiver because I haven't seen him since then. I got loads of abuse from the United fans after the goal. They were singing, "You Fat Bastard" and "Have you ever seen a salad?" The game ended 2-2 with Carl Shutt scoring the other goal and we kept our place at the top of the table, where we remained for the rest of the season

Mel STERLAND

We had a poor run towards the end of the campaign, winning just once in seven games. The game we won was a 4-0 thrashing of Sheffield United, who were also in the thick of the promotion race. When it came to the last day of the season, it was between us and Sheffield United for the title and we had to win at Bournemouth to be sure of winning it. On the way down to the south coast, I played cards as usual on the coach with Vinnie Jones, Mervyn Day and Imre Varadi. We played three-card brag and I won a grand off Vinnie but he had to owe it me because he didn't have the money on him. "I'll give it you, I'll give it you," he said. I'm still waiting now for the cash!

It was a red hot day at Bournemouth and there were thousands of Leeds fans who travelled down for the match. I wasn't fully fit because I'd got a slight hamstring problem, but there was no way I was going to miss that game. Carl Shutt was a sub that day and he was taken off after coming on because he was so exhausted. Chris Kamara put over a cross which was headed in by Lee Chapman to give us a 1-0 win, giving us the title on goal-difference.

The champagne was flowing on the coach journey back to Leeds and there was a lot of money at stake on the cards. I lost a couple of grand. Vinny Jones also lost a couple of grand and Mervyn Day probably won about the same amount. But we weren't bothered because we'd just become champions of the Second Division. It was a great day at the end of a fantastic season. Howard Wilkinson had predicted that we were going to win the title and he was right.

CHAPTER TWELVE

Title Joy And The Beginning Of The End

I was now a First Division player, earning good money and as a family we were enjoying life to the full. We had nowt when I was a kid, so I wanted my kids to have what I missed out on. They had everything they wanted and we had good holidays. When we went on holiday, we didn't go for just a week or two weeks, we went away for a month. We regularly went to America and we did it right, staying in good four-star or five-star hotels.

We lived in a large, detached house in Dronfield, just outside Sheffield, which was a great place for parties. When I had a party for my 30th birthday, we hired a marquee and got a couple of top local chefs – brothers Wayne and

Mel STERLAND

Jamie Bosworth – to put the food on. All the lads from Leeds came and there were some of my old Sheffield Wednesday team-mates. The lads had all chipped in some cash to pay for what I thought was going to be a strip-o-gram, but what they got instead was a snake-o-gram. There were two guys who came with a python and it frightened me to death, slithering round my neck. We had an indoor swimming pool and Carl Bradshaw decided to jump into it, bollock-naked. He didn't need any persuading to get his clothes off and jump in. The only problem was that he was so pissed that he didn't realise the cover was still on!

At another party, a friend of ours called Simon, who was a Leeds fan, decided to stay over. All the rooms were full of other guests, so he went upstairs to find a spare camp bed which was in the loft. We were sitting in the snooker room below, drinking and chatting, when suddenly the ceiling above us burst open, showering everyone with plaster. When we looked up, there was a fat lower leg, complete with sock and shoe, dangling through the hole. After Simon retracted his leg, I stood on a chair and shouted through the hole, "You big daft fat bastard, tha fucking paying for that!" I called him "Twinkle Toes" from then on.

Howard Wilkinson went out and signed some very good players like Gary McAllister, John Lukic and Chris Whyte in readiness for the First Division. McAllister was a great footballer, but I had my ups and downs with him. When we were playing Southampton at home and there was only about a minute left, we got a throw-in right in front of the dug-out which I took. "Macca" wanted the ball thrown to him, but somebody got close to him so I threw it to someone else. He threw his hands up in protest and as we were coming off the pitch I went over to have a word with him. "Macca, don't fucking do that in front of the manager," I said. "I'm sorry," he replied, "I was just frustrated that you didn't give me the ball."

John Lukic was a very good keeper, who'd done very well at Arsenal, winning I don't know how many medals. He was quiet and thoughtful, keeping himself to himself – it took him half an hour to answer a question! "Lukey" is a good lad, but a tight sod as well and that's why he's worth a few quid now with a string of properties. Imre Varadi was in the car with him once when he used his gold card to pay for a fiver's worth of petrol!

Chris Whyte was a very good defender who was known as "Huggy Bear" after the *Starsky & Hutch* character. I also used to call him "Malteser Head" because of his patchy hair and he used to say, "Stan, Stan, shut up!" in his Cockney accent. It was Howard Wilkinson who gave me the nickname "Stan" when I was at Sheffield Wednesday. When I was taking people on, I'd always try to get past them again and put a cross over, but I often failed to get the ball past the first man. "You're not Stanley Matthews," Wilko would say. When I did the same thing at Leeds, the same response came from Wilko. "I told you at Sheffield Wednesday, you're not fucking Stanley Matthews," he shouted. "Get it in the box early." After that, the name "Stan" stuck with the lads at Leeds.

Playing in the First Division saw me come up against Arsenal midfielder Steve Williams, who I'd had a run-in with previously. When I was playing for Sheffield

Mel STERLAND

Wednesday, Williams spat at me, saying that I'd cheated to win a penalty. I chased him up the tunnel at the end of the game but I couldn't get near him. When we were preparing to face Arsenal, Williams was still in my head after spitting at me and I was planning to chin him. I told John Lukic, who'd played with Williams at Arsenal, what I was going to do. Lukey was his mate and he warned him to get off the pitch as quickly as possible at the end of the match. As soon as the referee blew the final whistle, I went looking for Williams but he went off straight away so I didn't get a chance to give him a slap. I wish I could have got my own back because it was horrible to be spat at.

Another player I clashed with was Billy Whitehurst, who was an animal on the pitch.

Off the field, Billy's a nice guy and I used to go for a drink at a pub he later had in Sheffield, but he was a different man when he was on the field. He tried to bully you saying, "I'm going to fucking do you. When a cross comes in, I'm going to have you."

When Whitehurst was playing for Newcastle and Brian Marwood was at Sheffield Wednesday, Brian was telling everybody before the game that he and Billy were good mates from their time together at Hull City. "He'll not hurt me, Billy," he was saying. Well, nobody could believe it when Billy topped Brian, doing his medial ligaments and putting him out of action for about six weeks! Apparently, Brian's wife wouldn't speak to Billy after that.

I came up against Whitehurst when we played Sheffield United at Elland Road. We both challenged for the ball in the centre-circle and he did me, so I

Boozing, Betting & Brawling

stamped on him, which probably wasn't a good idea. In the second half, when Sheffield United had a throw-in down the right-hand side, Whitehurst came over to stand in front of me and I knew that he was planning to whack me in the nose. At that moment, I happened to look over to the dug-out and saw that Whitehurst's number was being held up to show that he was being substituted. He had his back to me and hadn't noticed the board, so I thought I'd tell him that he was going off. "Billy," I said, attracting his attention.

"What?" he growled as he turned round.

"Tha fucking going off, Billy. You've got to go mate, see you pal!" What a relief it was to see him go off.

Asa Hartford and Paul Ince were two of the other dirtiest players I came up against in my career. I had to have six stitches in my ankle when Hartford went right over the top during a match at Maine Road. In a game at West Ham, their side featured a young Paul Ince, who went over the top. I was holding my knee and Ince stood over me and said, "You fucking northern cunt, do you want some more?"

It was a surprise when Vinnie Jones was sold to Sheffield United early in the 1990/91 season because he did a great job for Leeds. A lot of players and opposition fans used to wind him up, but he just got on with his football, playing in midfield with David Batty, Gary Speed and Gary McAllister. We used to go out quite a lot at Leeds and Howard Wilkinson loved that because the team spirit was fantastic. I remember going into a nightclub once in Leeds when someone was trying to pick on Vinnie. He wanted to fight Vinnie and it was

Mel STERLAND

pissing him off. Vinnie just said, "Fuck off, or you're going to get hurt." The guy said, "Oh yeah, who's going to hurt me?" With that, Vinnie stuck a right hook on him and the kid hit the wall and slid down it. That was him done and Vinnie just carried on talking and dancing as though nothing had happened.

I had my testimonial match in November 1990. It had originally been planned for the end of the 1988/89 season but it had to be put back following the Hillsborough Disaster. Even though I was no longer a Sheffield Wednesday player, I wanted my testimonial to be staged at Hillsborough, but Ron Atkinson wouldn't let me have it there. He said, "You're playing it at Leeds. I'll bring a Wednesday team up to Elland Road." I don't know if Ron refused my request out of spite because of the fact that I turned down the chance to go back to Wednesday when he asked me. It was a good night when the match was played at Elland Road, but I didn't get a big crowd – there were only about 5,000 who turned out. I think if the game had been at Sheffield Wednesday, I'd have got a lot bigger crowd and that really gutted me. I'd worked hard and served the club for 11 years, but Lawrie Madden only did seven years and he got a testimonial. That hurt me as well because I think he got a crowd of about 15,000. No disrespect to Lawrie, but someone from the club could have turned round and said, "Hold on, Mel did 11 years here, he should have a game at Hillsborough."

I later got another testimonial when I was manager of Boston United, with Leeds sending a team to York Street. Des Walker, Gordon Strachan and Mark Bright all played in a Boston XI against a strong Leeds side which included a

Boozing, Betting & Brawling

number of first-teamers including John Lukic, Tony Dorigo, John Pemberton and David White. I was grateful to Howard Wilkinson for agreeing to send such a strong team, but it was pretty much a waste of time, with a crowd of just over 3000.

Gordon Strachan was in the veteran stage of his career, but he was still doing the business. I'd have no hesitation in saying that Gordon was the best player I ever played with. He just loves football and was so dedicated, the way he looked after himself. Gordon took seaweed tablets and he brought them in for the rest of the players to take. Most of the players were on them. I took them for about two days, but that was me done after that because they were disgusting. I still told everyone I was taking them, but I wasn't.

We did well in our first season back in the First Division, finishing fourth. We proved that we could compete against the top teams and we were full of confidence when we prepared for the 1991/92 season.

I wasn't fully fit at the start of the season because I was just coming back after a double hernia, which kept you out of action for six to seven weeks then. You'd be back playing after about 10 days now, which is unbelievable. We were at home to Nottingham Forest on the opening day and I didn't really think that I'd be involved. I'd trained after playing in a couple of reserve-team games and Howard Wilkinson obviously thought the time was right to ease me back by including me as a substitute. Wilko sent me out to get warmed up and I thought I was going to get on. He decided against sending me on though, so I sat back down on the bench. That went on a few times; I'd do a light job on the touchline, do some stretching and then sit down again. I saw Brian Clough in the away dug-out and noticed his face was red-raw, which was obviously due to drinking heavily. Wilko decided to keep me on the bench and when the full-time whistle went, I was heading for the tunnel when Cloughie came over to me and said, "Young man, well played, you were brilliant." I was so stunned that I struggled to think of what to say to him. Not only was the great Brian Clough talking to me but he was also congratulating me on my performance, even though I'd not played! "Oh, thank you," I finally spluttered. He'd obviously been on the whisky or something. That was the only time I ever spoke to Cloughie. As everyone knows, he was one of the great characters in the game and it was a shame that his drinking got out of control because he lost it towards the end of his time in management, as my experience with him showed. One of the Forest lads told me that people thought he'd packed up drinking, but he hadn't. He'd hide bottles of spirits in the garage, under lawnmowers and all sorts of places.

I came on as a substitute against Sheffield Wednesday at Elland Road. It finished 1-1 after Steve Hodge equalised for us following a goal from David Hirst. That was the first time I played against Wednesday and it was a strange experience after spending so long at Hillsborough but obviously I wanted to win for Leeds because they were paying my wages.

We hammered Southampton 4-0 at their place and I ran Micky Adams daft in that game after coming on as a replacement for the injured Chris Fairclough early on. Gary Speed, who got two goals that day, has scored a lot of goals for

Boozing, Betting & Brawling

a midfielder, often with his head. He has got a great leap on him to say that he's not particularly tall. When he jumps, he just seems to stay there. We got back from Southampton at 2.30am Thursday morning. People moan about playing several games in a short space of time but you just have to get on with it.

When we played Manchester United on the Saturday, I made my first start of the season. Fairclough wasn't fit to play so John McClelland switched to partner Chris Whyte in central defence and I played at right-back. We got off to a great start when Lee Chapman scored after only seven minutes. A lot of people used to think Chapman was a big lump but he scored a lot of goals. Ryan Giggs, who was only 17, came on and caused me a few problems. After weathering a lot of pressure, it looked as though we were going to hold on for a point, but Bryan Robson equalised just four minutes from time. The Leeds fans call Manchester United players and fans "scumbags". When I was at a Leeds game earlier this year, Allan Clarke saw a woman with a red coat on and said to her, "What are you doing with that on? We hate the scumbags."

"It's a red coat," she replied. He'd already had a go at me for wearing a red tie! I suppose I should have known better after wearing a green tie during my time at Rangers.

When we faced Arsenal, who were the defending champions, we came back from 2-0 down to secure a 2-2 draw following goals from Gordon Strachan (penalty) and Lee Chapman. I needed stitches after suffering a leg injury and was replaced by Steve Hodge.

I was fit enough to play in the 3-0 win over Manchester City. It was a game which featured a rarity – a goal from David Batty. It was a great effort from about 25 yards and the crowd went berserk because he didn't score many goals. He'd got a wonderful shot on him, packing a lot of power but he never used to have a go. He'd regularly shoot from distance in training and we'd ask him why he didn't do it in games.

Carl Shutt scored the only goal of the game at Chelsea the following week and I can remember him jumping over the advertising boards to celebrate with the Leeds fans. Shutty had only just recovered from an injury and Wilko decided to gamble on him. Wilko didn't tell Shutty that he was playing until late on because he couldn't cope with it. He used to get wound up so leaving it until later than usual to tell him gave him less time to think about it.

A goal-less draw at Coventry was largely forgettable. In fact, the only thing that comes to mind when I think about that game was how smelly Coventry winger Peter Ndlovu was! He's the smelliest footballer I've ever known, stinking of B.O. I told him that he stank, of course, to try and put him off.

Our unbeaten start to the season continued when we beat Liverpool 1-0 at Elland Road following a first half goal from Steve Hodge. I remember booting Steve McManaman. He was doing ever so well for Liverpool at the time and I knew I'd have to give him a kick. The ball was played over the top and it looked like it was going out for a goal-kick but McManaman ran after it and managed to keep it in play. After stopping the ball, he turned round to face me and I clattered into him. I hit him full on with a tackle and he ended up going over the advertising boards. I hurt him and he was quiet after that.

Boozing, Betting & Brawling

After a 2-2 draw at Norwich, we were second in the table when we prepared to play Crystal Palace at Selhurst Park. With leaders Manchester United in European Cup-Winners Cup action, we had a chance to close the gap at the top. Palace had to make an early change after John Salako was injured in a clash with me. As the ball was knocked over the top, I backed into Salako and he fell over, injuring his knee. It was accidental but he was hurt and had to go off. I don't think he was ever the same player again after that because he was plagued by injury problems. We never really got going in the game and went down to an injury-time goal from Mark Bright. The defeat left Manchester United six points ahead of us with a game in hand.

Next up was a Yorkshire derby at home to Sheffield United and it proved to be a seven-goal thriller. I had a hand in the opening goal, scored by Steve Hodge, after Blades defender Paul Beesley failed to deal with my throw-in. I added a second from a free-kick, which resulted in the Blades fans giving me loads of stick. They were singing, "You've never seen a salad." Another one was, "You fat bastard, you fat bastard, you ate all the pies." When Ian Bryson fouled Tony Dorigo inside the area, we were awarded a penalty, which set up an interesting exchange between me and Gary McAllister. I was the regular penalty-taker but McAllister had taken over the role in my absence when I was injured. When we were awarded the penalty, McAllister assumed he was taking it and picked the ball up. I wasn't having any of it though because I was desperate to take it, so I went over to him and started trying to wrestle the ball from his grasp. "Fuck off you fat cunt, I'm on 'em," he said, resisting my attempts to grab the ball. "Fuck off you Scotch bastard," I replied, "I'm taking it against these cunts, I fucking hate Sheff United." We were like two kids, fighting over a ball in a school playground! I felt under more pressure than normal when I finally managed to get the ball off McAllister because if I'd missed it, I'd have no doubt got a bollocking off Wilko. Fortunately, I managed to put it away, which prompted the Blades fans to give me more abuse about my weight. I couldn't resist taunting them by rubbing my stomach as I made my way back to the centre-circle.

After being 3-0 up at half-time, we looked set for a comfortable win when Hodge scored his second goal of the game early in the second half. Dave Bassett's men had other ideas, however, with Dane Whitehouse in particular causing problems for us. After Jamie Hoyland pulled a goal back, an ankle injury forced me to go off. Tony Agana then reduced our lead to two goals and Carl Bradshaw made it 4-3 in the 83rd minute following a poor clearance from John Lukic. That set up a tense finish to the game but we managed to hold on and win.

Following a 4-2 win at Notts County and a 1-0 victory at home to Oldham, Leeds went to the top of the table for the first time since 1974. In the *Yorkshire Post*, Howard Wilkinson was quoted as saying, "We have worked hard to get where we are; now we have to prove to everyone we are not one-hit wonders. Sometimes when a team gets to the top, people ask if they can stay the course. It is vital that we keep getting good results until Christmas, because we have played enough games now to be able to say to ourselves that, given a fair run of the ball, we can have a say in this title race."

We lost the top spot after the following game, a goal-less draw at Wimbledon, because Manchester United beat Sheffield United. I scored in a 2-0 win at home to Queens Park Rangers with a deflected free-kick, taking my tally to four for the season.

I scored again in the following game at Aston Villa, which was shown live on ITV. We won 4-2 to go back to the top of the table and I should have won the Man of the Match award after setting up two goals and scoring one. But because the decision was down to Gary Lineker, he picked a striker, Lee Chapman.

I came up against the tricky Peter Beagrie when we played Everton at Elland Road.

Beagrie was a good player but he could be frustrating because he'd beat a defender, then check back to try and beat them again. I felt sorry for the strikers he played with because they'd make a run, then have to come back to stay on-side and do it all again. You just had to kick Beagrie and that's what I did when I played against him some years before during his time at Stoke. I knew he'd had an injection in his knee before the game. Nigel Worthington got down the line, crossed the ball and Lee Chapman fouled keeper Peter Fox after he'd caught the ball. Fox didn't appear to realise that a free-kick had been awarded because he threw the ball out to Beagrie. I'd heard the whistle and thought it was the right time to whack him. I caught him with a beauty on his bad knee and I think they had to carry him off. He still mentions that incident when I see him now.

Mel STERLAND

After wins over Everton and Luton, we were a point ahead of Manchester United and two points ahead of Howard Wilkinson's Christmas target. We were held 1-1 at home to Tottenham, which was the start of four successive draws. After a goal-less draw at Nottingham Forest, we drew 3-3 at home to Southampton on Boxing Day. Steve Hodge scored twice after getting on the end of a couple of my crosses. Iain Dowie pulled a goal back for Southampton before Gary Speed restored our two-goal advantage, heading home another cross from me. It looked as though we were heading for a fairly easy win, but goals from Alan Shearer and Dowie meant we had to settle for a point. After the match, Howard Wilkinson described it as the most disappointing performance of his time at the club.

We went into the game at home to Manchester United knowing that defeat would put Alex Ferguson's men further ahead in the title race. Neil Webb gave them the lead with a controversial goal. TV replays showed that Ryan Giggs was in an off-side position and it appeared that Chris Whyte was pulled back by Steve Bruce. We were awarded a penalty 10 minutes from time when Gary Pallister fouled Gary McAllister. Gordon Strachan was on penalties at the time but he was struggling with a back injury so it was agreed that I'd take it. Along with rivalry between the two clubs, there was also the fact that defeat would have left us five points off the top of the table, so there was a lot going on in my head when we were awarded a penalty. I put it to Peter Schmeichel's left and he went the other way. Early in my career, I used to smash the ball straight down the middle when I was taking a penalty because, nine times out of 10, the goalkeeper dives left or right. I remember having a penalty saved by Charlton's Nicky Johns, who just put his arms up and knocked the ball over the bar. I'm surprised it didn't break his wrist, to be honest, because I hit it with such power. I had to vary things later on in my career and put it to either side because keepers would be tipped off about my habit of going for the middle of the goal

We went back to the top of the table on New Year's Day with a 3-1 win at West Ham after Manchester United suffered a surprise 4-1 defeat at home to QPR.

After losing 3-1 to Manchester United in the Rumbelows Cup, we faced Sheffield Wednesday at Hillsborough. I had a hamstring problem so I wasn't fully fit, but I still played. It was my first return to Hillsborough since leaving Wednesday to join Rangers and I received a good reception from the Wednesday fans. It was probably helped by the fact that I didn't leave Wednesday to go to Leeds. I got a little bit of stick but you're going to get that, whoever you are, when you return to your old club.

Goals from Lee Chapman and Tony Dorigo gave us a 2-0 lead before John Sheridan pulled a goal back for Wednesday with a controversially-awarded penalty. Gordon Watson dived after being challenged by Chris Whyte. It was never a penalty but referee Philip Don fell for it. The goal made little difference though because we battered them. Chapman went on to complete his hat-trick and further strikes from Mike Whitlow and Rod Wallace completed a 6-1 victory. It was the club's biggest league away win since 1930. With the win coming against Wednesday, there were some mixed emotions but I just had to do my best for Leeds.

Mel STERLAND

Manchester United knocked us out of the FA Cup, just as they'd done in the Rumbelows Cup, but we still had the edge in the title race. After coming from behind to draw 1-1 with Crystal Palace at Elland Road, we were relieved to hear that Manchester United had also only drawn at Notts County. Our next game was at home to County and I opened the scoring, meeting a Gordon Strachan corner to head my seventh goal of the season and the 70th of my career. Then I did my ankle following a clash with Mark Draper just before half-time. I won the ball but as I came away with it, Draper just caught me with his studs on my ankle. It was an accident; he didn't mean to do anything, but I knew straight away that I was in trouble. I wasn't able to carry on after the break so Mike Whitlow came on as my replacement and we went on to win 3-0 with David Batty and Rod Wallace also getting their names on the score-sheet. Incidentally, it turned out that my twin brother Glyn had a feeling at that time that I'd been hurt. Many times when I was playing football, Glyn would turn to someone and say, "Our Mel's got injured" and he said to his wife that day that he thought I'd suffered a bad injury. He'd not been to the game, but he turned out to be right because the injury ended up finishing my career. Glyn still does that sort of thing now because he knows when I'm poorly. It's unbelievable and quite scary really, but I don't get the same feeling with him.

As we prepared to travel to Oldham, Howard Wilkinson swooped to sign Eric Cantona. Sheffield Wednesday famously passed up an opportunity to sign Cantona after he did well in an exhibition match played on an artificial pitch. Everyone says it was Trevor Francis' fault but I was told it was the Wednesday

Boozing, Betting & Brawling

directors who insisted that they wanted to see him play on grass.

Cantona had his ups and downs with Wilko. He used to fake injury when he was only going to be a sub because he wanted to be playing, so he was a bit of a selfish bastard. When we played at QPR and he was going to be a sub, Eric turned round to Wilko and said, "I don't want to be a sub." So Howard decided to leave him out altogether, then gave him his passport and told him to go home. Eric got a taxi from the QPR ground, travelled all the way up to Leeds, got on a plane and flew back to France.

Eric was very quiet and came across as shy, keeping himself to himself. When he first came to the club I thought it was because he didn't speak much English, but I soon found out that he did understand the language. I was sat in the changing room one day with a copy of the *Daily Mirror* and he said, "Mel, you pass me the paper." He then sat there and read it.

There were lots of rumours that he was shagging the wife of one of the players. Every time I went out with the rest of the players for a beer, people would come up and say, "Is it true that Wilkinson sold Cantona because he was knocking off xxxxxxx's wife?" But I never found anything out regarding that.

One day when I was injured and in the changing rooms, Cantona came in and had a shower. He put this expensive Rolex watch by the sink and left it there, so I picked it up and gave it to Alan Sutton, the physio. Alan rang him up and said, "Eric, you've forgotten your Rolex watch." Eric wasn't concerned at all about the missing item. "Alan," he said, "if I lose my watch, I go out and buy another one." That showed just how much money he had because it must have been a fifteen grand watch. It turned out to be a big mistake when Cantona was sold to Manchester United, but I think Howard had had enough of him and he'd had enough of Howard.

X-rays failed to reveal the extent of the damage I suffered to my ankle against Notts County, so I carried on playing with the aid of injections and pain-killers, taking my place in the side for the Oldham game. It turned out to be a disappointing day as we lost 2-0 – only our second league defeat of the season – and slipped to second in the table.

A 1-1 draw at Everton was followed by a 2-0 win at home to Luton which featured Eric Cantona's first goal in English football. I was in the wars again when we played Aston Villa at Elland Road, having stitches put in a head wound after Cyrille Regis ducked and Chris Fairclough head-butted me. I went off to have the stitches put in, came back on with my head swathed in bandages and we got a penalty. I should have taken it but Gordon Strachan wouldn't let me. He thought I wouldn't know what I was doing after banging my head so he took the penalty and missed. It ended goal-less and we would have gone top if we'd won.

I was still playing on with the aid of cortisone and pain-killing injections. Charmaine would say, "You're not playing on Saturday, are you?" I'd say, "Well yeah, I perhaps will be playing because they're going to try and get me fit." I'd be sat with a bag of frozen peas on my legs to try and get the swelling down. After being given a cortisone injection, I'd play and do more damage to myself, without realising.

Boozing, Betting & Brawling

When I prepared to play in the following game at Tottenham, the Arsenal doctor came over to White Hart Lane and gave me a pain-killing injection half-an-hour before kick-off. I went off in the 70th minute and my replacement, Jon Newsome, scored one of the goals in a 3-1 win which took us two points clear at the top. That turned out to be my last appearance of the season as I was forced to watch the last 10 games from the sidelines.

We played Sheffield United in the penultimate game of the season and I was in the stand at Bramall Lane on crutches. I was loving it because we won 3-2 and it looked as though we were going to win the title. Manchester United still had to play so we had to wait for the title win to be confirmed. I was at home drinking champagne that day because I was confident we'd win it. A TV crew went to the house of one of the players where the likes of Lee Chapman, David Batty and Gary McAllister were gathered, waiting for the outcome of the Manchester United game. When the Manchester United game was over and we were confirmed as champions, the lads were drinking champagne. McAllister was fitted with an earpiece and as he was waiting to be interviewed, he spoke to one of the production staff off-air. "It's great to beat those red and white bastards," said McAllister. "That fucking red-nosed bastard Ferguson won't be happy about it." He was shocked when the message came back that Fergie was listening to him!

To celebrate the title win, we went on a victory parade around Leeds in an open-top bus. It was a great time and you don't forget days like that.

It was so frustrating being out of action towards the end of the season because I just wanted to play. I was having that much trouble with my ankle. I had pain-killers, put ice on it and had ultra-sound. It was the start of a nightmare.

CHAPTER THIRTEEN

It's All Over

I ended up having four operations on my ankle after a tendon came off the bone. I had the tendon stapled back on in one operation and everything seemed to be okay. But it came off again, so I went back and had it put back on. I managed to make my comeback against Blackburn on Boxing Day in 1992, which was my first senior appearance in nine months, but I only played about 50 minutes before coming off. I was in pain and had x-rays, followed by another course of ultra-sound.

I went to Harrogate to have the ankle looked at. The surgeon who performed the first two operations was called Mr Lawton and I had to see him at Leeds University. I used to go there with the Leeds physio Alan Sutton and one day when we were in the lift, I asked him if there were any bodies we could see.

Mel STERLAND

When he told me there were, I said, "Let's go and have a look." I just wanted to see what a dead body looked like and Alan agreed to take me into a room where the bodies were stored. We went into a large room and there was a terrible stench. There were hearts and other organs in various containers. I also saw a student standing by a trolley covered by a sheet. I went over to the student and said, "Is that a body under there?"

"Yes it is," he replied.

"Can I have a look?"

"Yeah, of course you can."

I wasn't prepared for what I saw though when he pulled the sheet back. I looked down to see the body of a man but there was half of his head missing. "What the ...." I shouted out, shocked at what I'd seen. I'd expected to see a full body and I was so freaked out by it that I ran off. Alan was used to that sort of thing and he just stood there, laughing his bollocks off.

I thought I'd beaten the problem after the fourth operation because everything was going really well. I was doing straight running with no twisting or turning and the physio gave me the go-ahead to work with the kids, so I joined in with them in training. Disaster struck when I got close to one of the kids, my boot landed on his boot and as he pulled away, it just twisted my ankle again. The pain was horrendous and straight away I knew that was it. I went to see a specialist and x-rays revealed the tendon had shredded so they had to remove it. It was the only bad injury I had in my career, but it finished me.

I was depressed and went on drinking binges. All I knew was football and

Boozing, Betting & Brawling

all I wanted to do was play. I was feeling sorry for myself and drinking heavily every night, even in the house. I'd be drinking all sorts of stuff like lager, vodka and Bacardi. I'd drink anything apart from whisky because I don't like that. My missus used to get mad with me, but I'd tell her to mind her own business and let me get on with my life. There were times when I'd go out at night and then drive up to Leeds and stay in my car in the car park, ready to go and see the physio for treatment the next morning. The security man, Jack, woke me up one morning. "Come on, you've got to go in and see Alan Sutton," he said.

People don't realise how depressed you get. I was drinking after the first operation, but not heavily because I'd got it in my mind that I was going to play again. But when I knew I wasn't going to get back, things got worse because I was worrying about what I was going to do next. Me and Charmaine grew apart for a while and it looked at one stage as though we were going to split up, but we never actually parted.

On one occasion I borrowed my brother-in-law Tony's car to go to Leeds after drinking the night before. I was still pissed and I hit the central reservation on the M1, just before Leeds. I'd drifted off, but that woke me and shook me up. I got into the car park, parked up, had my treatment and went home. There were big scratch marks down the side of the car where I'd hit the central reservation. I paid for the damage to be repaired, of course, but instead of owning up to what I'd done, I told Tony that Jack the security guard at the ground had put me close to another car in the car park and that the other car had scratched it. I only told him about three years ago that I'd fallen asleep at

Mel STERLAND

the wheel and hit the central reservation.

That wasn't the first time I risked getting caught drink-driving. Some years earlier, when I was at Sheffield Wednesday, I thought I was in trouble when I drove after drinking the night before, with the alcohol probably still in my system. I had a sponsored car with my name written on the side of it and as I was going down Sheffield Parkway, I looked in my mirror and saw a police car with its blue lights flashing, indicating that I had to pull over. "Oh God, it's still in my system", I thought, "I'm going to get done here". But I needn't have worried because all the copper said was, "Mel, can you get me some semi-final tickets?" Talk about relief. "How many do you want?" I said. Needless to say, I was only too happy to sort him out with however many tickets he asked for!

Just going to the club to have treatment was soul-destroying because I'd see the players go on to the training pitch and all I was doing was working with weights. Alan Sutton was very good because he worked me hard and just kept telling me to be patient, but I told him that I couldn't carry on like that.

When the inevitable happened and I was told I had to quit playing, it was the worst feeling in the world. I went to Harrogate to see the specialist, Mr Sephton, who performed the last two operations. He just said, "To be honest Mel, I don't think you can train full-time, so I don't think you'll be able to carry on being a professional footballer." It was in my mind that my time was up, but to be told that was devastating.

I went back to Elland Road and spoke to Howard Wilkinson, who was fantastic. Howard was like my father. When my dad died, he took me under his wing. He was strict with me, but he used to get the best out of me. After telling Howard that I was finished, I broke down and cried. There's nothing wrong with that, I've cried a few times. Howard put his arm round me and tried his best to console me. "Try not to worry about it," he said. "Hopefully we can sort something out."

I put my kit, boots and training gear in a black bin liner and headed home. When I got home, Charmaine was in the living room and I walked into there and dropped the bin liner in the middle of the floor. "Well that's it, thank you very much," I said as I stared at the bin liner. "You what?" Charmaine asked. "Are you not even going back next week?"

"No," I replied. "I've finished, I've done."

It was like walking straight into a brick wall and I felt lonely. I'd come to a crossroads in my life and I simply just didn't know which way to turn. I felt as though I'd been cast out into the wilderness and just told to get on with my life. Nobody came round to ask, "Are you all right, Mel?" I think help should be offered to someone when they've finished playing football. The PFA fund courses, but you've got to approach them for assistance. People like agents only want to know you when the going is good. When you're no good to them anymore, they just drop you like a ton of bricks.

The longer I was out injured, the more the insurance the club took out on me depreciated. I thought I was going to get about £250,000 because that was the figure Howard Wilkinson said he was trying to get for me as an insurance pay-out. We were going to pay-off the mortgage on our house with

Mel STERLAND

that money, but chairman Leslie Silver wouldn't agree to it. He said that out of the goodness of his heart, he'd been giving me appearance money, which was £1000 a match, while I was out injured. He said that I'd be paid a lump sum of £5,000 and allowed to keep my Mercedes. I finished up getting that and about forty-odd grand from money I'd paid into my pension.

The money I was on wasn't bad, but I just missed out on the real big money in football. I retired just when the Premier League started and *Sky Sports* started pumping millions into the game.

When I went back to Leeds to say goodbye to everybody, the lads presented me with a lovely Ebel watch worth about fifteen hundred quid. Unfortunately it later got nicked, which was a real sickener, especially as it wasn't insured. If anyone reading this has got an Ebel watch that says: "From all the players at Leeds United FC, all the best Mel" on the back, I want it back you thieving bastard!

When I look back, I think that perhaps if I hadn't had so many cortisone injections, I might have played longer. I think the players now are so powerful that they would refuse to do what I did, taking all the cortisones and pain-killing injections. The players are looked after more now than when I was playing.

After packing in playing, I didn't know what to do with myself. I simply had nothing to get up for, which was all new to me after getting up and training every day. As a player, you had to be at the training ground for 10.00am and you got used to the routine. When it stops, it's fair to say you're screwed up for a while. I know I certainly was.

CHAPTER FOURTEEN

You Can Bet On It

I've lost a hell of a lot of money since I started gambling as a 17-year-old at Sheffield Wednesday. It was another apprentice, a lad called Mick Bentley from Barnsley, who first got me into gambling when he took me along to Coral Bookmakers in Fitzalan Square in Sheffield, which is still there now. "Come and have a bet," said Mick. I told him that I didn't want to have a bet as I wasn't interested in gambling, but he persuaded me to go into the bookies and I had a pound on a horse, which won at 10/1. I thought, "Fucking hell, this is easy". I soon found out of course that it's not.

The amount I gambled increased as my career progressed and I used to gamble all the time. Gambling is a drug and you get a buzz from it. I've even lost some signing-on fees through gambling. My missus thinks the signing-on fees are in my pension fund, but they aren't.

I once bet ten grand on a horse – and lost. It was 2/1 and I thought I'd won, so I went out of the bookies for a moment and closed my eyes as I imagined picking up thirty grand. I then went back inside just in time to see my horse being beaten into second place, losing in a photo finish. I couldn't believe it because I could have sworn it had won. I was gutted. It was one of Henry Cecil's horses – he'd got two in the same race and he won with the outsider.

I'd got about half of the stake money for that bet by selling Cup Final tickets. That went off all the time; everybody used to do it. A tout would buy the lot off you and if it was Manchester United or Liverpool playing, you'd get about 20 times the face value. I was later banned from receiving tickets for 10 years and fined £250 for selling tickets. The sickening thing was, I didn't even get a drink out of it. A lad I knew gave one of the two tickets he received from me to an employee who then sold it on the black market. I found myself in trouble when the serial number was linked back to me. When I saw the lad who I'd given the tickets to, I said to him, "What about paying my fine?" But he refused to pay it and I don't even speak to him now.

When I was at Leeds, I used to go in and get perhaps £300 – £400 a day off my wages from the club accountant to fund my gambling. I'd go in and say, "Change us a cheque, Steve." He'd go barmy, but I just told him to stop being a mardy arse and then he'd sort me out. I'd write him a cheque out and if I won, I'd get my cheque returned and give him the money back, but nine times out of 10, I'd lose.

Boozing, Betting & Brawling

I also used to take part in card games – usually three-card brag – with the lads. The Sheffield United goalkeeper, Simon Tracey, used to come round to play, along with Martin Hodge and Imre Varadi. There were also a few of my mates who weren't in football. We used to take it in turns, going to different houses and there were some big stakes involved. When we were at my house, we'd play cards while some of the others played snooker. Charmaine would sometimes shout for us to stop when she could still hear the sound of snooker balls clacking at three or four in the morning. On one occasion, when there were about eight of us playing cards, we were all accusing each other of hiding cash because the figures didn't add up. To end all the arguments over whether someone was putting notes up their sleeve or whatever, we all agreed to strip off. Imagine the scene, eight blokes sat there at a table, bollock-naked in this house in a respectable area. If anybody had peered through the curtains, they'd have thought it was some sort of dodgy sex party! As it was, we were playing cards and because I was about four grand up, I was hoping that Charmaine would call a stop to the proceedings. Unfortunately, however, she left us to it and I lost the four grand plus two-and-a-half-grand of my own money.

My gambling once saw me get fined by Leeds physio Alan Sutton. When you were receiving treatment, you were allowed an hour at lunch-time. I thought I'd use the time to go off to the bookies, after first getting a cheque changed with the accountant for £300. I was supposed to return to the treatment room at 2pm, but the first race was at that time and the second was at quarter past. I had about a hundred quid on in the first race and my horse won, so I stayed for the next race and my horse also won in that one. I won about five or six hundred quid in total. When I finally returned for treatment, Alan wasn't happy with my time-keeping, saying, "You're late" as I walked into the room.

"I'm sorry Alan," I said, "I can't tell you any lies – I've been in the bookies."

"Well, I'd just like to tell you, you're fined fifty quid."

"Here you are," I said, pulling out a wad of notes from my pocket, "there's fifty quid there, thanks a lot, Al." I was more than happy to pay up after having such a good win.

I couldn't wait to finish training and have a bet. I'd be gutted when we had to go back in the afternoons because I just wanted to go to the bookies to get that buzz. A lot of it was down to boredom because of having so much free time. Some players liked to play golf or snooker, but I used to love going to the bookies and putting money on horses. I was also a regular at Napoleons Casino in Sheffield. I've had some good nights in there, but some bad nights as well. If I'm being honest, there have been more bad nights than good. I played blackjack when I was in the casino, nothing else. I never really bothered with the roulette, just blackjack.

I'd gamble on us winning when I was at Leeds. I used to go to Steve the accountant and ask him to cash me a cheque so I could put a bet on a few hours before we kicked off.

When we played night games at Leeds, I'd room with Chris Kamara and he used to go to bed while I went to the bookies. We stayed at the Hilton Hotel and there's a branch of William Hill just round the corner from there. We had to get

Boozing, Betting & Brawling

to the hotel for about one or two o'clock in the afternoon and go to the ground at about half past five. I could guarantee that before every night game, Kammy would be in bed and I'd be in the bookies. Kammy used to go barmy because when I'd lost all my money, I'd knock him up and borrow his cash card, which I used to get some more money to gamble with.

I think Howard Wilkinson knew I gambled, but he never said anything because it never affected me on the pitch. If I'd been in the bookies and lost two grand, it never affected the way I played. When I put that shirt on, I'd forget about it and go after my win bonus. That's how I used to look at it.

I'd bet on trebles back then. There are some great bets to be had now and if I was still playing, with some of the single bets you can have and no tax, there's a lot of money to be made. Obviously you're not supposed to do it now because you're not allowed to gamble. But I guarantee that most of the players who gamble have got their bets on in different names. It's not hard to work that out.

I went to different bookies rather than stick to the same one all the time because I'd get people coming up and talking to me about football. I'd be studying the form and you can't concentrate when people are interrupting you, wanting to talk about football.

One time when I had a football bet, I put a tenner on five draws. Four of them came up in the afternoon and I was waiting on West Ham v Liverpool in the evening. I was checking the score on Teletext and it kept coming up as 0-0. Then Julian Dicks got sent-off early in the second half and I thought it was the only game that was going to let me down, but it came up full-time at 0-0 and I was over the moon. I didn't know how much I'd won because I can't work out accumulators. I went to the bookies – which was at Crystal Peaks in Sheffield – and gave the slip to the cashier. "How much is that pal?" I asked.

"It's £5,750," he replied.

"Are you sure about that?"

"Yeah, positive, £5,750, but I can't pay you now."

"What do you mean, you can't pay me now? You took my tenner off me yesterday and now you can't pay me that money?"

"No, we've got to send the camera off, to see what time you put the bet on."

"Okay, I'll call for it tomorrow then."

So I went back the following day to collect the money. But instead of walking away with my winnings, totaling nearly six grand, I stayed in the bookies for the rest of the afternoon and did the lot in. I ended up going home with just fifty quid. Rather than reflect on the money I'd gambled away in the space of a few hours, I looked on the positive side after coming out of the bookies. "Well, I've won forty quid," I thought, reasoning that it had only cost me a tenner to put the bet on in the first place.

Being heavily into horse racing and gambling, I'd always wanted to own a racehorse. During my time at Rangers, we went to Villamore in Portugal for a family holiday. We were in a complex when I looked across and saw a guy I recognised, but I couldn't put a name to him. I sat down having a drink and when he came over, we got chatting. "What do you do for a living?" I asked him. He told me he was a jockey. "Oh, fucking hell, that's nice," I said. "I like a gamble, what's your name?"

"Micky Hammond," he replied.

"Bloody hell, you ride for Georgie Moore, don't you, up at Middleham?"

"Yeah, I do, but I'm retiring in a couple of years and I'm thinking of going into training."

It was like music to my ears when he told me he was a jockey. It made my holiday and got me thinking. I told him that me and my mates might be interested in getting involved in owning a horse and asked him to keep in touch. He promised he'd keep me informed and later, when he'd retired, he gave me a call. A mate of mine called Andy Hobson had already had a couple of horses before and he said, "Look Mel, I'm not having any more horses." But I started trying to persuade him. "Come on Andy," I said, "just give it a go with me. There are three of us involved in it." The third person was a Scottish guy I knew who'd expressed interest in getting involved in horse racing. I kept on at Andy and eventually he relented. "Go on then," he said, "let's go for it." After seeing Micky Hammond, the timing seemed right to own a horse. We left it to Micky to buy a horse and he went to the Doncaster sales. The one he went after was called "King Cracker" and it ran in a seller race with Frankie Dettori riding it, finishing second or third. Micky put in a bid of thirteen-and-a-half-grand and we got it. I got straight on the phone to Andy and told him about our new purchase. "We've bought a horse called King Cracker," I told him excitedly.

Mel STERLAND

Andy didn't share my enthusiasm, sounding less than impressed. "Fucking King Cracker? It doesn't sound very good that Mel, does it, King Cracker?"

"Well, you can't change its fucking name," I said, "that's what it is."

So we had this horse and it was stabled in Middleham, North Yorkshire. I used to go up to see it with Andy and our wives and the lad from Scotland also came down. It looked absolutely fantastic – until it went on a racecourse! Its first race was at Ayr and there was me, Charmaine, Andy and his wife Audrey who went up in the car to watch. Because we were so late setting off, the horses were already going round the parade ring as we drove into the car park. We'd travelled up in casual gear with our best clothes, which we were going to change into, in the boot of the car. Realising there was no time to find anywhere to change our clothes, I said, "Well, we're going to have to get changed here." It was so funny, looking at the four of us struggling to get changed in the car. All four of us were jostling for space, trying to take off and put on different items of clothing. Tits were out, cocks were out and clothes were all over the place!

When we finally got in the parade ring, King Cracker was there and he looked outstanding. The jockey was wearing the Leeds United colours of yellow and blue and everything looked to be set up for a good afternoon. I could hardly contain my excitement and I turned to my missus and said, "I can't believe we own a horse, this is fantastic."

Turning to Micky Hammond, I asked him what he thought about King Cracker's prospects. "Mel, it'll win," he assured me. "It's been going ever so well at home and it will win."

Boozing, Betting & Brawling

"Right, that means we're going to have a good bet," said Andy.

It was about 16/1, so Andy had five hundred quid each way, which was a lot of money then. I followed suit and it went down to about 10/1. It went behind the stalls and we were excited after hearing the trainer saying it was going to win. It got out of the stalls and was going ever so well. Three furlongs from home, we're already counting our winnings because it was absolutely cruising, but then the jockey gave it a smack and it tailed off and finished last. Obviously, we were absolutely gutted. We didn't get any prize money or anything and it had cost us a grand. Andy's going fucking barmy by this time. "He (Micky Hammond) said it was going to win," stormed Andy.

Micky said he was going to take it to Hexham, a couple of days later, where it would go over the hurdles. "It'll win there," he confidently predicted. So my missus, Andy and Audrey stayed up in Ayr in a hotel, while I had to go back down to Leeds to train. When Micky assured us again it would win, Andy said, "You said that last night and it finished fucking last." But Micky was adamant. "Yeah, but this is over the hurdles," he said, "it's got a great chance." With that endorsement, Andy had a good bet. I think he put a grand on again, five hundred each way. It was 20/1 and after I finished training, I went straight to the bookies and put two hundred and fifty quid on each way. I told everyone in the bookies that King Cracker was my horse and that it was going to win, so everybody in there backed it.

The race started and off they went. Three fences from home and again King Cracker was cruising. But two from home and the jockey gave it a smack on the arse and it finished last again. Well, I couldn't get out of the bookies quick enough because I think everyone in there wanted to kill me. And Andy wanted to kill Micky Hammond. "That's a fucking joke," said Andy. "The first time it never tried and the second time he told us it was going to win and it's finished last again." Micky protested, insisting the horse wanted gelding. But Andy hit back, saying, "Gelding? What about having its fucking throat cut? That would be a better idea!"

Owning a racehorse was just a bad experience because it cost us a helluva lot of money. Every month, it had some more new shoes. It must have had more shoes than my missus! To be honest, it got to the stage where I didn't dare ask Andy for the fees every month because he hadn't wanted to get involved in the first place. I used to send my missus round for the fees, which worked out at about four hundred quid a month. On top of that there were travelling expenses, the cost of the lad looking after it and the vet bills etc. We ended up selling it for sixteen hundred quid and we were just happy to get out. The sickening thing was that it then won at 20/1. You can't go into horse racing expecting to win money; you just have to view it as a hobby. If I won the lottery I'd probably have another dabble at it, but I'd have a proper racehorse and not a donkey!

When I first started gambling and I'd won about eighty quid or so, I'd buy clothes with the winnings, so I'd got something to show for it. But as I got older, I didn't bother about the money. I just wanted to try and win more and more. If I won fifty quid, I'd want to win a hundred. When I'd won a hundred, I wanted two hundred. My dad always used to say to me, "When you have a bet, go in and put your bet on and come straight out because once they've got you in there, they'll keep you in there." And I have to say he was spot on.

I see these players on massive wages who like to have a bet and I think, "Good luck to them." People had a go at Michael Owen the other year when it was reported he had a bet of forty grand. So what? He's earned that money. Forty grand? What's that to him? If he wants to gamble, good luck to him, he's not hurting anyone. He's not killing anybody or taking drugs. It's his money and he can do what he wants with it. I don't begrudge players who can earn big money. If the chairmen and directors want to give them five-year contracts and all that money, that's up to them.

I still gamble, but not as much as I did when I was playing. When I finished playing and the big money stopped coming in, I knew I couldn't carry on in the same way. If I could afford to gamble like I used to, I'd enjoy myself a bit more.

CHAPTER FIFTEEN

From Boston To Denaby

I spent a few months kicking my heels after packing in playing before taking up an opportunity to go into management. I didn't originally plan to get involved in management, but I'd really missed being involved in football, so when I heard that Boston United were looking for a new manager, I decided to put my name forward.

Boston were a non-league club at that time – playing in the Northern Premier League – and I thought it would be good to learn the job at grassroots level. The club had an impressive track-record when it came to managers because Howard Wilkinson and Jim Smith were both at Boston at the start of their managerial careers, so I thought it was an ideal place to go to.

I put in an application for the job and received a reply, asking me to go

Boozing, Betting & Brawling

along for an interview. When I went for the interview, I met the chairman, a guy called Pat Malkinson, along with the other directors. The club secretary, John Blackwell, was also there. We talked about my playing career and discussed what I would do if I got the job. After the interview, I was sat there talking to John while the chairman and directors went into another room. John, who has a bad twitch, was chatting to me about football and asking how I'd go about managing Boston. He was sat at the side of me and when his head suddenly went to one side, I thought the chairman and directors had returned – telling me I had got the job – and he was acknowledging them. I stood up to shake John's hand, turned round and there was no fucker there – it was his wicked twitch!

As it turned out, I did get the job, which was a great thrill. I was on two hundred and fifty quid a week, which wasn't bad at that level. One of the first things I did after landing the job was to contact Howard Wilkinson. Howard knew the club well from his spell in charge there and I thought it would be useful to talk to him. When I spoke to Howard on the phone, I asked him if he could give me any advice. "Mel, be honest with your players," he said. "Don't forget they are part-time, so they can tell you to fuck off because they don't need the football. It's just a hobby to them because they've got proper jobs. They'll kick you in the bollocks and let you down. Get them fit, get them organised and you'll enjoy it. It's a fantastic football club and the chairman's a great guy, so give it your best shot."

As someone who was new to the managerial scene, I knew that I needed some experienced back-up, so I brought in Ron Reid as my assistant. He'd been at the club before and jumped at the chance to return. I'd known Ron for a long time; he'd worked at non-league level with a few clubs and was a great coach. Ron's knowledge of the non-league scene was important because I knew nothing about it. I couldn't coach either, so Ron's help was invaluable. The way we worked was that he coached and I dished out the bollockings. It didn't take me long to realise that management was hard work, especially as the financial constraints meant we only had 14 players. It was good to be back in the game, although it took some getting used to the fact that we only trained twice-a-week, on Tuesdays and Thursdays.

The players were part-time, but I was full-time, although I didn't go to the club every day. I used my mobile phone to keep in contact with John Blackwell and Pat Malkinson. I had a good relationship with both of them. John is still at Boston after many years' great service and he works ever so hard. His wife Maureen also worked at the club. John did all the paperwork and sometimes he perhaps got too involved, but when people have got a football club at heart, they seem to do that.

As someone who'd always been involved in the professional game, I got the players thinking professionally. I made sure they were kitted out with club blazers, shirts and ties, so that they always looked smart on match days. We had a good first season, finishing fifth in the table.

At the end of the following season, we finished second, just a point behind Bamber Bridge. Their ground wasn't good enough to go up and we thought we

Boozing, Betting & Brawling

might get promoted to the Conference in their place. The club had to send details of their finances to league officials by a certain date, but somehow John Blackwell forgot to do it and that meant the club couldn't go up. Whether John had been told to forget to send the details in because the club couldn't afford to go up, I don't know. It was upsetting because Ron and I had worked very hard with the players and it really hurt us.

I received a letter in the summer informing me that my contract wasn't going to be renewed. I don't know if that was due to what had happened with off the field matters covered in the following chapter.

I had a good time at Boston overall. I can honestly say I did well for the club. They eventually got into the Football League and I can't help thinking that I might have taken them there myself if I'd been given the chance to carry on.

I had another spell in management when I went to Stalybridge Celtic, with Imre Varadi as my assistant. It was difficult because they were struggling in the Conference at the time and had players who were earning big money at that level. Some of them were on about three hundred and fifty quid a week and we couldn't get rid of them because they were under contract. We brought some players in, but things didn't improve and we got relegated. We had a meeting with the chairman and told him that we planned to arrange seven pre-season friendlies to raise some money. Using our contacts, we were going to play teams like Manchester City, Everton, Leeds, Sheffield Wednesday and Sheffield United. We thought it would be a good way to bring in some much-needed cash to fund some signings. What we didn't realise was that the committee were making plans for life without us because I received a letter informing me that our contracts weren't being renewed. I got on to Imre to tell him about the news. "If that's the way we're going to be treated, we're better off not being there," I said. We'd only been there about four months. It was a shame in many ways because we both enjoyed working at the club.

Howard Wilkinson was right when he warned me before starting out at Boston that players would not turn up for training sometimes. I'd ring up players who went missing. "Where the fuck are you?" I'd say.

"Why?"

"Well, you're supposed to be training."

"I didn't think we were training today."

They knew we trained on Tuesdays and Thursdays, but some of them just wouldn't bother turning up. That's why I decided that I didn't want to be involved in non-league management after leaving Stalybridge and I've never bothered since. I had enough of the hassle, to be honest, because it does your head in. A lot of people ask me if I'd like to go back into management, but I tell them I'm not bothered.

I also played non-league football for Denaby United and we won the North-East Counties League, which was fantastic. I couldn't join in with training because of problems with my leg, but it was a good laugh playing there because they were a great bunch of lads.

During my time at Denaby, I was round at Charlie Williamson's house, having a few drinks with a number of people including Imre Varadi and a lad

Boozing, Betting & Brawling

I know called Mick Cunningham, who is a chiropodist. We'd all had a few drinks when I suddenly thought that it would be a good idea for Mick to treat my feet there and then. Since we were all quite pissed by this stage, Mick was reluctant, before finally giving in and agreeing to do it. With everyone gathered round, Mick worked on my feet, cutting my in-growing toe-nails while pissed up! Everything seemed fine after that and we carried on drinking, but I was in pain when I sobered up. The nails had been cut back too far – it looked like David Blunkett had done the job! The following week, Mick came with Charlie to see me playing for Denaby. During the game, I went over to take a throw-in and as I leaned back over the fence to launch my big throw, I spotted Mick in the crowd. I immediately dropped the ball, marched over to where Mick was standing in the crowd, pointed at him and shouted, "You, yer cunt, I haven't been able to walk since you did my fucking feet!" I then turned round, took the throw-in and ran off, leaving Mick receiving perplexed looks from the crowd. I should stress that Mick is actually an excellent chiropodist – when he's sober!

I haven't been offered any jobs in football since leaving Stalybridge and I think that a lot of that is down to the fact that I had a brush with the law during my time at Boston. I was charged with handling stolen goods after a Post Office safe was found in my garage. Being accused of that was a shock to the system and obviously attracted a lot of unwanted publicity. Even though my innocence was eventually proved when the charges were dropped, mud sticks.

CHAPTER SIXTEEN

Safe In The End

"Are you Melvyn Sterland?" asked one of the two people who stepped out of a car parked outside my house.

"Yes," I replied, "have you come to look at the house?"

"No, we're police officers and we're arresting you on suspicion of handling stolen goods."

That was the start of two months of hell for me and my family, during which I feared I might be sent to prison for something I hadn't done.

On this particular day, I'd taken the kids to school and then took Charmaine to the hospital because she'd got a pot on her wrist. After that we went shopping before collecting the kids from school and returning home, where we found a car parked on the drive. Our house was up for sale at the time and I thought it was someone who had come to look at it. When they introduced themselves as police officers and told me I was being arrested, I said, "What are you fucking on about?"

"Anything you say will be taken down and may be used in evidence against you," the policewoman said.

To say I was shocked would be an understatement. Struggling to take everything in, I invited the police officers into the house, took the kids upstairs out of the way and then returned to speak to them. They repeated that I was being arrested on suspicion of handling stolen goods. I asked them what I was supposed to have taken but they wouldn't tell me. They said I had to go down to the police station for questioning. So they took me to Bridge Street police station in Sheffield, searched me and took my shoes off me before I was taken to a cell. I was sat in this cell not knowing what I was supposed to have done.

That day I should have been playing for Sheffield Wednesday old boys at Wolves. My mate Andy Hobson was ringing me on my mobile, but I'd not got it. He was trying to arrange for me to be picked up to be taken to Wolves. It was when Wolves were playing a night game and the match I was due to play in was in the afternoon. But instead of putting my boots on for a kick-about, I was in a cell instead, shitting myself because I didn't know what had gone off.

My solicitor came and told me they'd arrested Charmaine as well and she was also taken to Bridge Street police station. She was dressed up to the nines, looking absolutely fantastic, bless her. It was terrible for her because she's got a fantastic family. Her dad's probably never even seen a police cell or anything like that. The police quizzed Charmaine about various things for four hours before releasing her without charge. "How much did Mel have on him today?" they asked her. "About forty or fifty quid," she replied.

The police then came to me and told me what she'd said. "Yeah, that's about right," I said.

"But when we arrested you, you'd got two hundred and fifty quid on you," they replied.

"Well, before I picked my kids up, I had fifty quid on a dog which won at 4/1, winning me two hundred quid, plus there was my fifty quid stake. I think it might have been the 3.29 race at Crayford." Obviously, they went and checked it all out and found that what I'd said was true.

Without any warning, I was eventually taken to an interview room where these police officers started asking me questions. "Look, we've found this safe in your garage, do you know anything about it?" I was asked. "To be honest, I don't know what you're on about," I told them. I explained how I'd got up in the morning, taken my kids to school, driven my wife to hospital and then gone shopping before collecting the kids from school and returning home. On the same day I was questioned, the police interviewed someone who worked as a cleaner at our house and asked her if she'd heard anything.

I learned that the safe was from a Post Office in Dore, a suburb of Sheffield, only a short drive from our house in Dronfield. According to the police, whoever broke into the Post Office and nicked the safe put it in my garage in the early hours of the morning. "Well, in the early hours of the morning, I'm in bed asleep, not knowing what's going off and not knowing what's in my garage," I replied. "When I'm asleep, I'm asleep."

The police claimed four people had been in the garage, but there were supposedly five piles of money. One of the coppers looked at me and said, "That must have been yours." I said to him, "Haven't they got any mates then, who they're going to give a share to?"

I'd not got a key to my garage door, so it was open all the time, never locked. I was able to prove that because I'd been robbed and the insurance wouldn't pay me out because of the fact that I hadn't got a key to the lock. There were all sorts of things in there including a sit-on lawn mower and they took the lot. I bet there was stuff worth about eight or nine grand that went.

The house was up for sale and the police went all the way through it, looking for things, which wasn't very nice. When I was being questioned, much was made of the fact that the house was on the market. "Your house is up for sale and you need the money," one of the policemen said. "We can see you've had a horse and greyhounds, which you've no doubt lost money on." After seeing a photograph of me with some greyhounds, which was framed and on display at my house, they presumed that I'd owned the dogs. The photo was actually taken at Owlerton Greyhound Stadium in Sheffield during a race night which was organised as part of my testimonial year.

The police interviewed me again about three or four times and I was held in a police cell. I knew a copper at the station and thought he was a good mate of mine. He was a miner when I was at Sheffield Wednesday and when the miners' strike was on, I used to give him food and get match tickets for him. He came into the cell where I was being held and said, "Sterland, I want you." So I just sat on my bench and thought, "You can fuck off". Again, he said, "Sterland, I want you." I still sat there, refusing to budge, until he said, "Mel, I want you." I then got up and followed him into the interview room.

"What the fuck are you doing?" he said. "You're looking at 15 to 20 years."

"For what?" I replied. "What have I done wrong?"

"Just think of Charmaine. Think of Nathan and Chantelle."

"Look Alan, I don't know what you're on about. By the way, are you still seeing that bird at Ecclesfield?"

With that, he stood up and shouted, "Get back in that fucking cell."

There was one bobby who was quite good to me though, to be honest. He passed me a 'paper to read, but when he went, another copper took it off me. All I could do to try and keep myself fit was do sit-ups in my cell. I was in a cell for two nights and it was terrible. I don't know how these people go on when they get a long sentence.

When I first went to court, there were a load of TV cameramen and Press photographers waiting outside my house. Professional golfer Mark Roe lived opposite and some of the photographers were in his garden, waiting for us to come out. There were also a lot of reporters, photographers and cameramen waiting outside court.

The story made headlines in the local and national Press. The headline on the front page of the *Sheffield Star* on 9 February 1995 read: "Ex-Owl Faces

Boozing, Betting & Brawling

Raid Charge." Paul Whitehouse wrote: "Sheffield soccer star Mel Sterland was today charged in connection with a £63,000 Post Office raid. The former Owls and England star was arrested by detectives investigating a break-in at Dore Post Office." The report went on to say that I'd appeared at Sheffield Magistrates Court – accused of handling stolen goods – and that I was bailed to appear back at court on 9 March. Two other men were charged with burglary of a safe and its contents. The break-in had been discovered two days before the story came out. The safe apparently contained £28,000 in cash, along with stamps and documents worth thousands more. Police had recovered around £26,000 of the money.

A few days after I was released on bail, I played in a charity football game for Johnny Quinn's All-Stars at Herringthorpe in Rotherham. One of the lads in our team was former Sheffield Wednesday player Gordon Simmonite, who I've known since I was about 13, playing for Sheffield Boys. Gordon, who also turned out for Blackpool and Lincoln City, joined South Yorkshire Police as a police officer after finishing playing football. After hearing at work that I'd been arrested, I later found out that he was apprehensive about seeing me as he made his way to the game. Gordon was wondering how I'd be with him, knowing that he was a copper, after what I'd been through. He says that he really didn't know what to expect.

Gordon was late in getting to the ground and dashed into the changing room about five minutes before kick-off, with his boots slung over his shoulder. He was the last one in so it was a full changing room and he saw I was sat in the corner. I was bending down, tying my boot laces, when I heard the other players greeting Gordon. I looked up, caught his eye and said, "Hey, Simmo, I don't like fucking breakfast at your place!" All the lads were laughing and Gordon enjoyed it as well because he thought it was a great "ice-breaker".

It was a terrible time when I was on bail and all my family were very upset about it. I'd go out with Charmaine and you could see people looking at us and nudging each other, but we just got on with it. When I was in Josephine's Nightclub one night, I saw this guy looking at me in the gents and thought to myself, "Here we go". When I opened the door, he must have thought I'd gone out, but I hadn't. Talking to someone next to him, he said, "There's that Mel Sterland, who robbed that bank." I just had to laugh and bite my tongue because I was on bail. If I hadn't been on bail I'd have probably flipped and chinned him. When the guy came out of the toilets, I couldn't resist going over to him and putting him straight. I tapped him on the shoulder and said, "It wasn't a bank, it was a Post Office."

When we went out for a meal, there were four people on a nearby table who were gossiping about us. We overheard one of them say, "How can they afford to come out for a meal when they're going to court for robbing a Post Office?" Then when we went into a popular pub called the "Woodstock Diner" and walked towards the bar, everyone turned and looked at us. Me and Charmaine had to be strong at that time and not shy away.

Howard Wilkinson was fantastic during that time. I had a bit of stick from the lads who'd say things like, "Have you got any postal orders?" One night I was

Boozing, Betting & Brawling

out with Charmaine and there was a woman we knew who said, "Have you got any stamps?" I thought to myself that the first line of defence was attack, so I hit back by saying, "No, I haven't got any stamps, but we found your pension book in there and you're not the age you say you are." She got the right hump with me and just fucked off. She was giving it out, but couldn't take it.

It was a horrible time for us all, but fortunately we had some good friends around us, who helped us to get through it. Thanks to Phillip and Janet Knowles, I also had a good solicitor called Stephen Parramore who worked at Foy & Co and also got some references from some high-profile people in the game like Bobby Robson, Jack Charlton, Howard Wilkinson and Viv Anderson, which I've still got.

The case lasted about two months and it was hell during that time. My kids were in private school which was a good thing because I think if they'd been to a state school, they would have got absolutely murdered. Nathan went to Westbourne, which was where Howard Wilkinson's son used to go and Chantelle went to an all-girls school called Brantwood. Both sets of teachers were fantastic because they kept talking to Nathan and Chantelle about the situation.

When the case went to Sheffield Crown Court, my solicitor said, "Don't worry about it Mel, just have a smile on your face when you go into the court." And I did as he said because I was innocent. I knew nothing about what they found in my garage. But it was still one of those situations where I thought, "Fucking hell fire, I've been roped into something here. It could go either way, even though I'm innocent and I know nothing about it. I could be looking at 15 years."

I didn't have to go to court again because the charges were dropped the following day. Woodseats CID forwarded the facts of the case to the Crown Prosecution Service who decided there was insufficient evidence to prosecute. My solicitor rang me up and said, "We've got some great news for you. It's been thrown out, you're no longer on bail and you're a free man." The relief was incredible because it had been a nightmare. The pressure could easily have split up my marriage, but we got through it.

The headline on the front page of the *Sheffield Star*, 11 April 1995, read: "End of My Nightmare." The story, which was written by Bob Westerdale and Lisa Salmon, told of my relief after it was revealed that police were to formally drop charges against me. "Ecstatic former Sheffield Wednesday international Mel Sterland, cleared of involvement in a £63,000 Post Office raid, said this afternoon: 'This is the best day of my life. We have been to hell and back...but my true friends helped enormously by standing by me. This is a greater thrill than playing for my country'."

Boston said they'd stand by me when the story first broke, but it wasn't long after when I lost my job there. I will be forever grateful to people in the game like Howard Wilkinson, Dave Bassett, Trevor Francis, Danny Wilson and Viv Anderson for their encouragement during that difficult time. Even though I was innocent, there was always a lurking doubt in my mind that justice would go wrong and I'd end up in prison.

CHAPTER SEVENTEEN

On The Big Screen

I don't think anyone would have me down for being a thespian. In fact, I couldn't even spell the word without referring to a dictionary! But one of my claims to fame is that I have appeared on the big screen with famous Sheffield actor Sean Bean.

Sheffield film director Jimmy Daly came up with the idea of a semi-professional footballer being given the chance to play for his boyhood team, Sheffield United.

Sean is well-known for being a big Sheffield United fan – with a "110% Blade" tattoo on his arm – so he was the obvious choice to take the lead role in the film. It was originally going to be called *Pint o' Bitter*, but by the time it was released in 1996, it had been given the title, *When Saturday Comes*.

Mel STERLAND

Even though he supports that other lot from across the city, I've got a lot of time for Sean because he's a great guy. He calls into my local pub when he returns to Sheffield and his mum and dad also drink there, so I know the family really well.

To add some authenticity to the production, me and Charlie Williamson were approached to advise on the football scenes. We went to Hallam FC, a non-league club in Sheffield, where they wanted to film something. When we turned up at the ground, we saw this guy I know called "Botty" who was chasing all over the pitch, trying to keep a ball up in the air. I turned to the production guy and said, "What the fuck's he doing here?"

"Oh, we want someone to keep the ball up," he replied.

I went up to Botty and told him his services were no longer required. "Oi, fuck off," I said, "you're not doing this. They want someone to keep the ball up, not keep chasing after it. Go on, bugger off."

We got Charlie Williamson's lad, who was only a young kid, keeping the ball up. I was then asked to get more involved in the film. The production guy then said, "Why don't you be the captain of Sheffield United?"

I pointed out that I'd only gone along to show them a few things, like what happened in the changing room and so on, but they weren't deterred. Jimmy Daly said, "Come on Mel, be the captain". But I wasn't at all keen on the idea. "Fucking captain of Sheff United? No chance," I said. Sean Bean then had a go. "Come on Mel, you'll have a good laugh."

I eventually agreed to take the role, but the only way I was prepared to wear

Boozing, Betting & Brawling

a Sheffield United shirt was to put a Sheffield Wednesday one on underneath. Sean was laughing and pointing at me in the red and white. I then found myself saying a few words in the film. It was great, but it was hard work. We were at Bramall Lane from seven in the morning until seven at night, which was knackering, but it was a good laugh and a great experience. Sean had to take a penalty in the film and I had to work with him on his technique for a couple of days at the Pinegrove Social Club in Sheffield. He's a great actor, but crap at football, so I had to spend ages with him, demonstrating how to strike the ball.

Sean wasn't the only well-known star who appeared in the film because the cast also featured Pete Postlethwaite and Emily Lloyd. Pete, who's been in films such as *Brassed Off*, *The Usual Suspects* and *Jurassic Park*, was brilliant. He was one of the lads who loved a laugh and a joke. But I can't say the same for Ms Lloyd because she was a horrible bitch. She was a right stuck up cow who didn't mix with anyone. Nobody liked her because she used to look at everybody as if they were shit. A coat she wore in the film was given to my missus by the girls who sorted out the clothes.

The film premiere was at a cinema in Sheffield and a limousine arrived at our house to take me and Charmaine to the screening. We were given the red carpet treatment and there were loads of VIPs there, so it was a memorable evening. Charmaine describes it as one of the best nights of our lives and I think she's probably right.

It's fair to say I got a bit of stick from my mates for appearing on film in a

Mel STERLAND

United shirt and I still get ribbed about it even now. I'll go into the pub and one of the lads might say, "He's here, the Unitedite." My usual response is to say, "Fuck off, I'm no Unitedite. I had a Wednesday shirt under the red and white one anyway, so bollocks."

I was the manager of Boston at that time, so most of the players used in the film were Boston players. We all had to sign an agreement saying that we wouldn't get any royalties. It would have been nice to have had some royalties because the film has been on TV loads of times.

I got about fifteen hundred quid for my involvement in *When Saturday Comes*, so it was well worth it, although the money didn't last long. In fact, it lasted about five furlongs!

CHAPTER EIGHTEEN

"I'm Your Friendly Fish Man"

After packing in football, I didn't know what to do to earn a living because all I knew was football, but I was desperate to work because I've always been a grafter. I didn't claim any benefits for about four or five months and people used to encourage me to go on the dole. "Why don't you sign on?" they'd say.

"Because it's embarrassing," I'd reply. "They get you in there and ask all these questions."

"Listen, you should sign on. You've paid your dues and your taxes. In fact, you've probably paid a lot more than some of the fuckers who're claiming."

My wife was working, so she used to keep us, which was very hard for her.

Mel STERLAND

One day I decided to go to the benefits office. I was handed some forms to fill in and then signed-on, which was the most embarrassing experience ever. I used to try and get there when the office opened at 9am, in the hope that nobody would see me. As soon as the door opened, I'd go in, sign my name quickly and hurry off, but I did get recognised sometimes. People would say something like, "What are you doing here, Mel?"

"I'm not buying fish and chips am I?" I'd reply.

I'd receive a giro for about £80 every two weeks, which was a massive come-down from what I was used to. I signed on for a couple of months, but I didn't like it one bit.

I was looking at the job section in the *Sheffield Star* one day when I saw what I assumed was a driving job because it mentioned "delivery" in the job description. I didn't mind the prospect of doing a bit of driving so I applied and received a reply inviting me along for an interview. When I got there, after finding out it was a frozen fish company, I was asked to fill in an application form and the guy then asked me if I could report for duty the following day at 8am. I told him that I'd be there and left the place feeling surprised at how easy it had been. I went home and told my wife that I'd got the job. "Oh, that's good," she said. "It'll get you out of the house so you'll not be bored and you'll be earning money."

I had a good night's sleep and got up at about 7.15am, feeling as fresh as a daisy. After taking a shower I then had some breakfast before setting off to work in my new job. I arrived at the place, which was an industrial unit only down the road from where I lived, about 10 minutes before I was due to start. There were some nice new vans there and I was looking forward to starting work. A guy came over to me, introduced himself and said, "Are you ready for today?"

"Yeah, I can't wait," I replied, thinking I was going to be driving.

"Well, you'll be with me today," he explained.

I was a bit surprised when he told me that I'd be going out with him because I thought all I was doing was delivering some frozen fish. I'd got my driving licence and wasn't put off by the prospect of getting in a vehicle I'd never driven before. I thought all that I needed to know was where I was delivering to. The guy told me to get in the passenger seat because he'd drive.

We went just a few miles out of Sheffield and headed towards Dronfield, where I used to live. We were on my old road when he said, "Right, we'll just go on this road." I wasn't happy about that because everyone knew me there and I thought I'd look like a right twat. "Just watch me, Mel," my new colleague said, "this is all we have to do, it's so easy." We pulled up outside this house and I stayed inside the van as he got out, clutching a brochure, before walking down the path to the front door of the house and knocking on the door. I watched as a woman opened the door and then he spoke to her briefly before the door was slammed shut. "Fucking hell, what's going on here?" I thought.

The guy got back in the van and tried to make light of what had happened. "No problem, Mel," he said, "we'll try another one." After driving a short distance and pulling up outside another house, he got out and walked down the path to the front door again. I thought this time that I'd wind the window down so I could hear what he was saying. He rang the doorbell and when a woman answered the door, he came out with his spiel. "I'm your friendly fish man, what fish would you like today?" he said.

"Not today," the woman said, shutting the door before he could utter another word.

As he walked back to the van, I thought to myself, "I know what's coming next" as he opened the door to get back in the driving seat. I knew he was going to ask me to have a go and there was no way I was going to do it. I wanted to work but I didn't want to do that. We again drove a short distance, pulled up outside a house and this time, instead of getting out, the "friendly fish man" turned to me. "Right, you've seen me do it, now it's your turn," he said.

"Yeah, I've seen you do it and I've seen you get the fucking knock-back twice," I said. "You know that pub down the road, the Coach & Horses?"

"Yes," he replied.

"Drop me off there. I don't want this job. I'm not a friendly fish man. I thought I'd be delivering fish, not selling it door-to-door."

It was the shortest time I've ever been in a job. When I told him that I wasn't interested in the job, it was probably only about 40 minutes after I'd started. After being dropped off at the pub, I rang my wife and said, "Come and pick me up."

"Ooh, you've finished early," she said, "did it go well?"

"No, I've got my P45. I'm not working for them."

Boozing, Betting & Brawling

When Charmaine picked me up, she laughed her head off when I told her what the job entailed.

I've tried loads of jobs. I worked in a power station, dealing with asbestos, which I didn't enjoy. I had to go high up, which I don't like. Also, because it was a tight space, I felt closed in. I had to climb through a small hole and then slide along on my knees before I was able to stand up. It was horrible because you could look down the shaft and see how high up you were. I went in first, ahead of three other lads. When they followed me, I freaked out when I looked down. "What's up, what's up?" they said.

"Get out," I demanded.

"You can't get out."

I was going crackers. "Get out or I'm going to fucking kick you out," I shouted. I would have kicked them out as well because I wasn't happy at all, but they did get out. I got the job through my mate Angus, who managed the company, and another mate, Andy Hobson, who owned it. I had to go on a course to learn all about asbestos because it's deadly stuff and that was quite interesting, but the job didn't last long.

I sold photo-copiers and phone systems for a company in Sheffield called Concept after a lad called Austin Fitzgerald gave me a chance. I used to play in some charity football games and Austin was watching one time when Andy Hobson collared him. "Oi, you little fucker," he said. "Why don't you give my mate a fucking rep's job?" It was an unusual approach, to say the least! But Austin considered the proposal for a moment and agreed it was a good idea.

Mel STERLAND

"Mel's a local lad who's well-known," he said. "I'll offer him a job."

I went to where Concept were based in Sheffield, had a chat with Austin and he gave me a job. Selling was hard work. I knew nothing about phone systems and I knew nothing about photo-copiers. I had to learn about the industry, so I went on a couple of courses and picked it all up. I was given a company car and I enjoyed going out and meeting people. But doing cold-calls, phoning companies listed in a directory, was difficult. I'd sometimes ring up and speak to someone who turned out to be a Sheffield United fan. I rung one bloke up and went through the usual introduction. "Hello, it's Mel Sterland from Concept, can you tell me how many phone lines and extensions you have?"

"Well, I don't give a fuck how many lines and extensions I've got, how long's a piece of string?" he replied before putting the phone down.

He was obviously a Unitedite who thought it would be a laugh to have a go at me. I shouldn't have done it, but I got my own back. I dialled 141 before phoning him – so it would withhold my number – and then gave him a mouthful when he answered. "D'ya know you, you're nowt but a fucking wanker!" I said before slamming the phone down. Funnily enough, I don't think we did any business with that particular company!

I did that job for about 18 months. My name opened up a lot of doors and I think Austin did very well out of it. I'd get Sheffield Wednesday fans wanting to talk to me about football.

I did cold-calling, trudging around streets with the rain pissing down and thinking, "What the fuck am I doing here?" The thing was that I did it; I've never

Boozing, Betting & Brawling

been afraid of grafting.

I then worked for a company called Energas, who were also in Sheffield, selling industrial gases. A lad I knew called Jacko worked there and his boss was a big Leeds fan. I went for an interview, got the job and was told to cover Rotherham and Doncaster. That was disappointing really because I wanted to cover Sheffield, but they'd already got somebody covering the area. I'd go cold-calling, asking what kind of gas they were burning. I enjoyed the work and stayed with Energas for about nine months.

You've got to have plenty of front to be a sales rep, which I don't mind. I just don't like it when people are being ignorant and slam doors in your face. I wouldn't do that myself. When people come round to my house trying to sell something, I never slam the door in their face. I always listen to them because I know what it's like. I'll give them a chance and if it's not what I want, I'll say something like, "Not today."

I went from being paid big money at Leeds to earning about twelve grand a year as a sales rep and sometimes less than that if I wasn't picking good deals up. When your income drops significantly like that, you have to adjust and stop doing certain things. For example, I couldn't go into the betting shop and have a hundred quid bet. That had to stop.

When you're earning big money, you think it's going to be coming in all the time. You think it's never going to stop; you think it'll be there until you die, but it doesn't work like that. It's difficult to stop yourself spending money when you're used to having it. I'd pay for things by credit card and when the bills came in, I'd think, "They'll get paid". But you've got to have money coming in to pay them. We ended up running up massive debts and it was a frightening time. When I was out of work and being chased for money, I'd ring companies up to ask for extra time to pay off my debts. "Can I give you twenty quid?" I'd say. They'd agree to the request because at least they were getting something.

When I finished playing football, my kids were still in private school, which was very good. It wasn't cheap – Chantelle's school cost about eleven hundred quid a term – but we scrimped and saved to keep them there. It wasn't my kids' fault that I'd been forced to pack in playing football, so I was determined that their education wouldn't suffer. Nathan initially went to the same school as Howard Wilkinson's son. We had to pull him out of there eventually because we got to the stage where we couldn't afford it, but we put him into another private school. My kids had to adjust to a different level and they managed to do that quite well. Our Chantelle did ever so well at school, getting some good results. Nathan didn't get the best grades, but he tried his best and now he's grafting, earning a living at Debenhams department store.

Some time before the court case, there was a story in the *Sheffield Star* saying that I'd not been paying the mortgage on my detached house in Dronfield. I'd got an agent called Jerome Anderson and he had a mortgage advisor who was supposed to have sorted everything out regarding the mortgage. But he forgot to send the forms in for the direct debit. Even now, I don't know what's in my bank account. I know what goes in, but I honestly don't have a clue how much is in there. One day a reporter from one of the Sunday tabloids came to

Boozing, Betting & Brawling

my house and asked, "Is it right you're in arrears with your mortgage?" I refused to talk to him and was later told that someone from the same newspaper had rung up the lenders, pretended to be me and was given all the information they asked for on the mortgage. They were informed that the payments were five or six months in arrears, which was all down to the advisor failing to send the forms in. The problem eventually got sorted and the outstanding amount was paid.

Eventually, however, we did have to leave our house for the simple reason that we couldn't afford to carry on living there. With the money I had been earning from football no longer there, we got to the stage where we just couldn't keep up the mortgage repayments. The house wasn't repossessed, as some people thought, but we effectively had to give it up. We handed the keys in and paid Eagle Star ten grand to get them off our back because the debt had been bumped up by the interest they were charging. Eagle Star had asked for fifteen grand, but they were informed by our solicitor that if they didn't accept our offer, I'd go bankrupt and they wouldn't receive a penny.

Most people make money out of property, but we lost a fair chunk on that house. We paid £230,000 for it and probably spent another £30,000 on doing it up. We didn't get a penny back when we handed the keys in and Eagle Star sold the house for £175,000.

It was an absolutely fantastic house, with four bedrooms, swimming pool, sauna, snooker room and a bar. Outside there was a double garage, courtyard and a quarter of an acre of land. It was a beautiful place so it was a real wrench to leave.

Mel STERLAND

We needed to quickly find somewhere to live so we rented my father-in-law's three-bedroom semi in the Handsworth area of Sheffield, not far from where I was brought up. It was a blessing that my father-in-law wasn't living in the house when we needed a place because if it hadn't been available, we'd have probably been looking for a Council house, which would have been very difficult after what we'd come from.

We ended up living in that house for about six years. Then after saving up some of the money I earned from working in sales jobs, we were able to buy a detached house a few miles away. We weren't in it long before we bought another place in Handsworth, where we live now.

I was looking for a change of direction in my working life so when an opportunity to get involved in a football agency came up, I jumped at the chance. It appealed to me because it was obviously a way of being involved in the game to a degree. A mate of mine called Steve Penistone, who is a financial adviser, chatted to me one day and asked me what I was doing. "I'm selling gas," I said.

"Bloody hell, Mel, you should be doing something better than that," he replied. "Have you ever thought about being a football agent?"

"Well, I've obviously thought about it, but I've not been pushed into it."

"Right, well come and see me and we'll have a chat."

I went round to see him and after discussing a few ideas, we decided to set up an agency, calling it Premier Sports UK. We had to go down to London and sit exams, which we both passed, to earn our FIFA licences. It was Steve's role to look after things like the players' mortgages and pensions, which is what I think all good agents should do. They need to ensure that all their clients have to do is concentrate on playing football and our company tried to do that.

My job was to attract players and get them signed up. With my experience of playing football, I was also able to guide them in the right direction. For example, I'd advise our clients against taking risks with their health like I did when I was playing. I told them to let nature take its course when they'd got an injury, rather than taking cortisone injections. Otherwise, they could end up having health problems later in life, like me. In my day, all they wanted to do was get you out on the field and I felt under pressure to play when I perhaps shouldn't have played. Like the daft bugger I am, I didn't object when I was told that I was going to be given a cortisone injection. I wanted to play because I loved to go out there, perform for the fans and do well. In the current game, with the power the players have, managers know they can't push players into playing because they'll just turn round and say, "Up yours, I'm going to get myself right. I'm not going to play with an injury."

I'm now paying for playing when I should have been resting because I'm in so much pain and I'm absolutely knackered. The pain is unbelievable at times, especially when it's cold. I didn't want to see other players risk their health so I'd tell them to learn from my experiences. "Just get yourself fit," I'd tell them. "Don't let the manager or the physio push you into playing before you're ready because you'll suffer in the long run."

A lot of people say that footballers don't need agents, but I think it's important for players, especially the younger ones, to have someone to talk to and to act on their behalf. I think back to when I signed my first contract at Sheffield Wednesday. I felt intimidated facing Jack Charlton and there was no way I was going to negotiate with him. I think it's important that players have a good, honest agent. A bent agent might be a good friend of a manager, which could work against a player. The manager could have a word with the agent and say, "Get him to agree a cheaper deal and we'll look after you."

A lot of agents are crooks and a lot of managers are too. The sooner the managers are caught out the better because the game is so bent. I've only really known that since I became an agent. I never thought under-hand deals went on when I was a player because I never came across it, but you hear loads of things when you talk to people in the game. They tell you about certain managers who are "looked after" by agents when it comes to transfer deals. It's difficult to prove that, of course, but I know for a fact that it does go on in all the divisions. Certain managers are rewarded by agents when they sign players attached to them. A manager might get in touch with the agent and say, "I've signed this player and told him to join you, where's my reward?" When I was working as an agent, if a manager asked me for something out of a deal, I told them where to go because it's not right.

I tried to strike up a working relationship with certain managers who wouldn't have anything to do with me. They basically told me that they had their own agents who they dealt with, which was disappointing. Managers can also put pressure on players by telling them that they've got to be tied to a certain agent.

Boozing, Betting & Brawling

I hope that it all comes out eventually and the managers and agents who are involved in the dodgy dealings are named. The sooner the FA deals with the problem properly, the better it will be for football.

When I decided to pack in working as an agent in 2003, Steve carried on running Premier Sports UK. I enjoyed my time with the agency, but it was frustrating at times because most players were already tied to agents, making it difficult to add to our list of clients. We didn't try and poach players who were already attached to someone. I wished I'd gone into the agency business as soon as I stopped playing football because the time would have been right to get hold of players.

CHAPTER NINETEEN

Clot Could Have Proved Fatal

I agreed to help out a mate by doing some labouring for him, but I couldn't do anything because my leg swelled up. Feeling a recurring pain in my right ankle, I took a couple of Ibuprofen pain-killers as usual to ease the pain and thought no more about it.

Then one day my shin was getting bigger and Charmaine took one look at my leg and said, "That's a blood clot." I went to see the doctor, who asked me what I thought the problem was. When I told him that I thought it was a clot, he said, "I think you're right." The doctor said that he was pleased I'd gone to see him because it could have been fatal if I'd just carried on and ignored the problem.

Boozing, Betting & Brawling

I was rushed into the Hallamshire Hospital in Sheffield, where they carried out a series of tests. I thought I was only going to be in there overnight, but they ended up keeping me in for 12 days and then nine days the second time. At one stage I was fighting for my breath and couldn't breathe. I have a blood clot in my calf and it turns out that it went to my lung. The doctor said it must have been on my lung from when I retired from playing. It's frightening to think it was there all that time because I used to play in charity games. If the clot goes to your heart, they can't do anything for you; it's goodnight. It was a very frightening time for me and my family.

Fortunately, they managed to get rid of the clot on my lung, but I've had a few health scares since. I thought at one stage that I'd had a heart attack because I felt a tingling sensation down my side. They kept me in hospital overnight before I was given the all-clear. I was put on medication and it looks like I'm going to be on it for the rest of my life. I'm on Warfarin – which thins the blood – and I have to take around 12 milligrams a day.

I only have to walk about 10 yards and I get cramp in my shin and my groin. I used to run around like a nutter when I played football, kicking anyone who moved, so it's frustrating now when I get out of breath just walking upstairs. I can't do the travelling that I'd like to do either because of my health. When I drive, I sometimes have to get out for a stretch. I'll pull up, get out and stretch my groin. I see people looking at me, wondering what the problem is. I must look like a right nutter at the side of the road!

My health problems obviously mean there's no chance of me taking part in

Mel STERLAND

charity football games. Even if I did feel fit enough to play, it would be out of the question because I'm not allowed to participate in contact sport. I'd bruise easily if someone caught me and that could clot. I'd love to play in the Masters games involving ex-pros which take place every year because it'd be great to meet up with some of the old players and have a laugh. Paul Allen, who is involved with the PFA and organises the Masters, always gives me a ring and asks me whether I'm available. When I tell him that I'm still struggling, he says, "No problem, Mel. When you're available, you can play." The problem is that if I'm ever given the all-clear to play at some point in the future, I'll probably be too old and too fat!

The clot is on my right leg, where I had my four operations. I think that the problem stems from having been given cortisone injections and pain-killers to play football. Proving that is another matter. I'd be given cortisone a few days before a game and then pain-killers just before kick-off. When you're running around and getting kicked during a game, you don't feel a thing because it's numb. You don't know the damage you're doing to yourself at the time. It's two or three days later when you think, "Fucking hell fire, that's killing me." I must have had a helluva lot of cortisone injections during my career. At one time I was being given one cortisone and one pain-killer every week and I think you're only supposed to have about three cortisones in a lifetime.

I thought that I may have been in a position to make a claim for compensation for negligence relating to the use of cortisone. I spoke to a Sheffield-based lawyer called Garry Dickinson – who I've known for many years

180

— and he advised me that I could have a case for medical malpractice. Garry was then at EAD Solicitors, who won a number of other football-related cases. We went to see some of the top surgeons in the country, with the investigations going on for three years, and at one stage it looked as though we had a strong case. But when proceedings were about to be issued, the final surgeon we spoke to said he couldn't say, hand on heart, that the injections were definitely to blame for bringing my career to a premature end. I've got to say that EAD Solicitors did everything possible to try and help me. I'm very grateful to Garry and his colleagues because they worked very hard on my behalf and refused to charge me. That was a very generous gesture because I'm told the costs had mounted up to many thousands of pounds.

I wondered whether specialists feared saying my problems were down to the injections because of the likely repercussions if they did. If I had been given the encouragement to go ahead with the case, it could have led to many other footballers making compensation claims.

There's a time-limit for taking legal action so nothing will happen in my case now. But I'd love it if it was proved that the over-use of cortisone was the reason for other ex-players suffering health problems. I've seen various former players around the same age as me who are also having problems. I bumped into my old Leeds team-mate Peter Haddock a while ago at a game. He had to retire from playing due to a bad injury and I asked him how his knee was. "Mel, it's absolutely fucked," he said. Like me, Peter blamed his health problems on the injections he was given. Incidentally, Peter's doing really well with a parcel courier business and that's a line of work someone suggested to me because you can earn some good money at it. I'd love to give it a go, but I just couldn't do it because the driving would be too much for me.

I have to accept what I can and can't do because life goes on and I just have to get on with it. They can't take the clot out of the main artery in my leg because another one could come and go wherever it wants to go and then it's "Roy Orbison". In other words, over!

I've been told to be patient and keep taking Warfarin. I have to go to get my blood count checked every week. It needs to be between two and three – anything over that figure means that my blood is thin. If it goes really thin, blood can come out of my nose or wherever. I might be taking Warfarin for the rest of my life, which is a pain in the backside, but if it's going to keep me alive, it's got to be done.

CHAPTER TWENTY

Boozing & Brawling

On the outside, it appears that I'm fine because I like having a laugh, but inside I'm rotten and I think a lot of that is due to my health problems. I turned to alcohol when my problems got me down – just as I did when I was forced to quit playing – and I was drinking heavily for four or five years.

I was drinking at home during the day and then going to the pub at night. I was easily drinking 20 pints of lager every day, which is a ridiculous amount to put away. Not only that, I'd also drink shorts such as Bacardi and Coke and Vodka and Orange. I'll drink most things except whisky, which I don't touch because it makes me puke.

All my mates noticed how much I was drinking and they tried to help, urging me to cut back. But all the pleas fell on deaf ears because I refused to accept that I'd got a problem. "There's nowt wrong with me," I'd say to anyone who told me to get some help. Eventually, however, it just got to the stage where I thought, "Hang on, there's something wrong here". I told Charmaine how I felt and she encouraged me to get some professional help.

In 2006, I went to see my GP and told him that I wanted to see somebody who could help me with my drinking problem. He referred me to a Psychologist called Manjeet and I went to his surgery every week for a while. I felt a bit awkward when I went to the surgery because I used to see people in the waiting room who knew me, but I knew I had to go through with the treatment. I told Manjeet everything about my life, how I'd lost my mother at quite a young age and things like that. I'd never really talked to anyone about my problems before, not even Charmaine.

I felt great after talking about my problems because it was like a weight had been lifted off my shoulders. I saw Manjeet on about six occasions and when it came to talking about my excessive drinking, Manjeet asked me if I wanted to stop drinking.

"No, I don't want to stop drinking because I know I can't do that," I explained. "I think I'd be even worse if I stopped drinking completely."

"Well, what do you want to do?" he asked.

"I want to control my drinking."

"Well, I'd advise you to go to Alcoholics Anonymous."

He gave me the details of an organisation called the Sheffield Alcohol Advisory Service, based on Abbeydale Road. I booked in to go there but I wasn't

Boozing, Betting & Brawling

looking forward to going because I thought everybody there would know me and I didn't want people knowing that I had problems with drink. I saw a lady at the centre and she was absolutely fantastic, asking me about my drinking habits. She made notes and I asked her whether I'd be able to have a one-to-one meeting rather than be put in a group with other people who had drink problems. She assured me that wouldn't be a problem and said that I'd be contacted within a week. They got in touch with me and I returned to the centre for a one-to-one session with a counsellor called Bryan. He was magnificent, asking me how much I drank and what I wanted to do. "Well, I don't want to pack in drinking totally, I want to control it," I told him. He then asked me to write down what I drank on a daily basis. I told him that I could drink 20 pints of lager, as well as shorts, without a problem. I could drink that amount in a day and not have a hangover the next day. "Well, if you don't feel bad the next day, you've probably got a problem," he said. "I want to see you in a week's time and in the meantime, I want you to write down everything you drink." I came out of the place feeling brilliant again. It was great to be able to talk to someone I could trust about my problems. I wrote down what I drank over the following seven days and I didn't drink as much as I normally did. When I went back for another session with Bryan, I handed him the list of what I'd had to drink, which he looked at as soon as we sat down. "You're not an alcoholic," he said.

"Why's that?" I asked.

"Because looking at that, you're not drinking a lot."

"But I'm drinking."

"Yes, but you're not drinking every day."

"That's because I'm trying to control it."

"Well, if that's what you're drinking, you don't have to come here anymore, but I'd like you to come."

I agreed to carry on going for treatment and I cut down my drinking a helluva lot. Sometimes my kidneys were killing me and Bryan advised me against stopping drinking completely. "If you stop drinking, your organs will wonder what's happening and you could be in serious trouble," he said. "You have to cut down and control your drinking."

I had about five sessions with Bryan until I felt that I didn't need his help any longer because I'd controlled my drinking. A lot of people don't know what to do to get help when they have problems with drinking. I can only advise anyone who is having a problem controlling their drinking to go and receive professional help. I felt great after I'd spoken to first Manjeet and then Bryan. It did a lot of good to talk to them and take on board the advice they offered.

I love a drink and I don't think I'll ever stop loving it. I still drink a lot, probably about 12 or 13 pints in a session, but I'm not drinking every day and I feel as though I've got it under control.

When I was a footballer, I used to get a lot of hassle when I went out drinking. I still get people having a go at me now when I'm out and about, but it happened more when I was still playing. For some reason, footballers are often targeted by people who've had a few drinks. I'm generally one of the most placid blokes you could meet, but I'll fight anybody if I'm pushed.

Boozing, Betting & Brawling

I was out with a few of my mates in the centre of Sheffield one night when one guy decided to have a go at me. There was Bryan, Robert, Angus, "Salty", "Waggy" and Darren Gray, who we call "Eddie". We'd had a laugh and a few beers before going to a take-away for a kebab at the end of the night. While we were waiting in the take-away, this lad with long, greasy hair, tied in a pony-tail, came over and started having a go at me. "You pig," he said.

"What's up with you?" I replied, looking straight at him.

"You fucking Wednesday bastard."

"There's no need for that pal, I'm out with the lads having a quiet drink."

"I'll fight you for twenty quid."

Bryan, who's a sensible lad, turned round to this guy and said, "What gives you the right to talk to him like that?" Everybody just burst out laughing when he said that because it sounded funny, but the guy who'd been having a go at me didn't think it was funny. Instead of just walking off, he repeated his challenge to fight me. "Come on you piggy bastard, I want to fight you for twenty quid," he said. I was skint at the time and didn't even have twenty quid, to be honest. I wouldn't have been out that night had it not been for the fact that my mates had generously paid for my drinks. I was getting pissed off with the guy by this time and told him that I'd take him on if he increased his offer.

"Make it a hundred," I said.

"No, twenty quid," he said.

"Make it a hundred quid and I'll fight you."

He refused and walked off, but I wasn't going to leave it at that because he'd got me so revved up that I couldn't get him out of my head. He'd embarrassed me in front of my mates and they all wanted to knock him out. I told them not to bother, thinking that if anyone was going to knock him out, I wanted the satisfaction of doing it. Shortly after he'd headed off into the night, I thought, "Right, I'm having him" and went after him. I saw that he'd walked past the Grosvenor Hotel and I followed him. I didn't just sneak up and hit him from behind, I gave him fair warning before I struck. As I approached him, I said, "Hey, big mouth." He turned round and ran at me, charging like a bull with his head down. As he came at me, I fired some punches into his head and he went down on the ground. I then stooped over him, grabbed his pony-tail and started smashing his head on to the pavement. "Make it a thousand pounds, you fucking idiot," I screamed at him as his head struck the concrete. I must have bashed his head against the pavement several times and blood was pouring from a gaping wound, going all over my shirt. Then my mate Rob, who's a big lad, came over and kicked him straight in the back. With the guy rolling around on the pavement, groaning and clearly badly hurt, both of us panicked, suddenly worrying that we'd done some serious damage to him. We decided to leave the scene as quickly as possible and flagged down a passing taxi. As I headed home, all sorts of things were going through my head as I replayed the incident in my mind. How seriously injured was the guy I'd fought with? Was he still alive? When the taxi dropped me off at home and I went inside the house, Charmaine was obviously shocked to see me in a blood-splattered shirt and wanted to know what had happened. "I think I've killed somebody," I said to her.

"You what?" she said with an anguished look on her face.

"I think I've killed somebody," I repeated. "He embarrassed me in front of my mates, challenging me to fight for twenty quid. I just lost it and gave him some fist."

We decided to go away for a few days and ended up staying with some friends in London. Fortunately, it turned out that I hadn't killed the guy, but I was seriously worried for a while that I had. It was nice, to be honest, to have given him some pain. He just had to have it. The guy wanted to fight me for no reason and he got his comeuppance.

On another occasion, I was out with Imre Varadi one Thursday night when we were both playing for Leeds. We'd been to a presentation night in Sheffield and afterwards we decided to go to a place called the Curry Centre on London Road. We didn't drink because we were due to be playing on the Saturday. After sitting down at a table, Imre got up to go to the gents and I started looking at the menu. I had a feeling that someone was looking at me, so I glanced over the top of the menu and saw a bloke, who was sat with another guy and two women, staring at me. "You fucking clown," he mouthed to me as I caught his eye. I presumed the "clown" comment referred to the expensive, multi-coloured shirt I was wearing, but I ignored him and carried on reading the menu. When Imre returned to the table, I warned him that it was probably going to kick off. "Imre, I think we're going to have some bollocks in here tonight," I said.

Mel STERLAND

"Why?" he replied.

"Well, one of those kids to your right has just called me a clown."

Imre turned round straight away to look at the bloke who'd had a go at me. "And you're a clown as well," the guy said to Imre. "Here we go," we thought as we looked at each other.

When one of the guys came over towards us, Imre thought he was about to stick one on him, so he got up and hit him. When the other guy came over, I got up and took a swing at him, but he ducked and I ended up hitting the owner of the restaurant! I felt like a right twat because the place was full of people and I've ended up hitting the owner, who I knew really well. I then grabbed the bloke I'd tried to punch and started slamming his head into the wall. Imre chased the other guy into the kitchen, forcing several startled staff to jump out of the way as he started kicking and punching him. Imre, who'd got new leather-soled shoes on, slipped on the shiny tiled floor as he tried to connect with a punch and his fist missed the guy's face, plunging straight into a large saucepan full of mulligatawny soup instead! He was there with soup almost up to his elbow. Fortunately, they'd only just put the saucepan on the stove, so it wasn't very hot.

The guy I'd been fighting didn't know what day it was by this time because I kept bashing his head against the wall and he was in a daze. Imre then came back out of the kitchen with the guy he'd been fighting, who was holding his battered face. Imre had hold of him and he marched him towards me. "You better fucking apologise to my mate," Imre said to him. After he apologised, his bird came over and aimed a kick at me. Protecting myself, I put my foot up and struck her shin, which would have been a red card offence if I'd have been playing! She fell down holding her shin and then started having a go, saying that she was going to sell a story to the newspapers. "I'm going to tell the *News of the World* what you've done to us," she said. "Well, do what you want," I replied.

Imre and I apologised to the owner of the restaurant and offered to buy a drink for all the people in the place for the inconvenience, but he insisted that it wasn't our fault. We told Howard Wilkinson the following day what had happened in case there was any comeback and he was fine about it. I was told later that the guys we clashed with were big-hitters in the Sheffield United hooligan gang known as the "BBC" (Blades Business Crew), but I don't know if that's true.

I was in a pub called the Woodthorpe Arms in Sheffield when I got in a spot of bother through no fault of my own. I was out with my mate Andrew Hobson and I'd had quite a lot to drink, but I wanted to carry on. When I suggested going to the Woodthorpe Arms, Andrew said that he didn't want to go there. "Stay away from pubs like that, they're a waste of time," he said.

"I'm going down there with a few of the lads," I replied.

Andrew said that he was going home and that proved to be a wise decision because a fight broke out when we got in the pub. I wasn't involved in the fighting but some twat threw a bottle and it hit me straight in the face, breaking my nose. I went to the hospital to have it sorted out and everyone took the piss out of me when I reported for training at Leeds a couple of days later because, with two black eyes, I looked like a panda. Howard Wilkinson realised that I hadn't done anything wrong; I just found myself in the wrong place at the wrong time. In some ways I was lucky really because the bottle could have hit me in the eye and if that had happened, there's a chance I'd have been blinded.

If I'm being honest, I can't have been easy to live with over the last few years. There have been plenty of times when I've been moody and refused to listen to anybody, resulting in arguments with my wife and kids. A lot of it is down to frustration because I can't do a quarter of what I used to be able to do. One of my lungs is damaged and that's why I get out of breath so easily.

I was prescribed anti-depressant tablets to help me with my depression and they have helped tremendously. Cutting down on my drinking has also made me feel a lot better and I can talk to people now instead of shouting at them. I do have bad days and if I've not taken my anti-depressants, anything can happen. I've taken two tablets a day for a few years and I don't think I'll ever come off them now. If I haven't taken them, Charmaine knows straight away. Our Chantelle can also tell and it's got to the stage now where, if I'm being moody, she asks, "Have you taken your tablets?"

It's funny how things work out. When my health problems got me down and it again got to the point where I was thinking about whether it was all worth it, I became a grandfather. Chantelle presented me with my first grandchild on St Patrick's Day in 2004 when she gave birth to Leon. He takes a lot of things off my mind because he's a great little kid and I'd be a heartless bastard if I did anything now to hurt him. It's not only him I'd upset, of course, but the rest of my family and my friends.

CHAPTER TWENTY ONE

No Regrets

I consider myself lucky to have been paid for doing something I loved, working in the fresh air and travelling the world. I wouldn't have been able to travel the world if I hadn't been a footballer.

Many former players struggle to adjust to life after football, some more than others. My old England team-mate Gazza is a good example of someone who has lost his way after leaving the game. Much of it is down to missing the routine and the camaraderie, which you don't really get in any other working environment.

As I've said previously, I was lost for a while when I first left the game, but I don't miss playing now. I enjoyed everything I did as a player, but I accept that it was a part of my life that's over. I miss having a laugh with the lads but I don't

Boozing, Betting & Brawling

actually miss playing football one bit. I'm lucky in that way because I think part of the problem with poor old Gazza is that he still thinks he can play.

There are no constraints on me now so I'm free to do what I want. I had to watch my weight during my playing career, meaning I had to be careful about what I ate and drank. You get to the stage in life where you want to go out and enjoy yourself. The one day of the month as a player I miss is pay-day!

I don't miss the hangers-on you attract when you're a well-known footballer. We had a lot of money when I was at my peak and we used to spend it. There was always a party going off and it was always us who were putting it on and paying for it. We had very few friends and a lot of acquaintances, but at the time you think they're all your friends. It's only when you look back you realise that wasn't the case. There are plenty of people who want to be around you when you're making the headlines and earning the big money, but where are they when you've finished playing? They all go on the missing list and you never see them again. I can count on one hand how many real friends have stood by me and Charmaine through thick and thin, but our real friends were still there even when we hit rock-bottom.

Before my health problems prevented me from playing, I used to turn out in various charity football games. A former Sheffield Wednesday player called Johnny Quinn organised matches featuring various old players, one of whom was Emlyn Hughes.

Emlyn, who lived in Sheffield, was one of my favourite players when I was younger and it was great when I got invited to play alongside him for Johnny

Mel STERLAND

Quinn's All-Stars. I was like a little kid again, looking up to my hero. Emlyn was a lovely guy who'd do anything for you and his fitness was incredible. When he was at Liverpool, Emlyn would wear a bin liner in training to make him sweat more and he also played for us wearing a bin liner. He'd then join all the lads for a couple of pints after the game. Emlyn would come out with some great stories from his career and we all had a great laugh. Sadly, Emlyn died from a brain tumour at the age of 57 in 2004.

Johnny Quinn ran the team for years and should get an MBE for the amount of money he raised for various charities. Johnny decided to end his involvement with the team in 2006 because he's no spring chicken and he decided that he'd had enough. After the old players who were involved in Johnny Quinn's All-Stars had been out on a Christmas do, they asked me if I wanted to take over from Johnny. At first I turned down the offer but then I spoke to one or two people a couple of days later and agreed to do it. That meant that the name of the team was changed to Mel Sterland's All-Stars. Dave Barker from DB Sports agreed to act as a sponsor and provided us with nice new kits.

Gordon Simmonite, who was at Sheffield Wednesday when I was starting out, does all the organising and I basically just lend my name to it. Gordon arranges the games and I turn up on the day, watch the game from the sidelines and sign autographs. Ernie Moss, who played for a number of clubs including Chesterfield, helps Gordon with the organising. Ernie's fitness is incredible. He's 58 but he runs every other day and looks as fit as a fiddle. When you see how much he does in a game, he runs about as if he's 21. All the lads who are

Boozing, Betting & Brawling

involved in Mel Sterland's All-Stars deserve a lot of praise because they all do it for nothing, paying their own travelling expenses. We tend to play about six games a year and have raised thousands of pounds for various charities. I wish I could play in the games but at least I can join in with the banter. It's like being a young player again, mixing with your mates and having a laugh.

As well as Gordon and Ernie, the players who turn out on a regular basis include Kevin Pressman, Greg Fee, David Pugh, Lawrie Madden, Bob Newton and Imre Varadi.

There are various other players who play when they can including Tony Cunningham, John Gannon, Keith Curle, Chris Wilder and David Hurst.

We raised about £17,000 for a girl from Rotherham who has an incurable disease when we played a game at Rotherham United's Millmoor ground last year. The Chuckle Brothers, who are from Rotherham, were involved that day. They want sectioning, by the way, because they're mad! They only talk to you out of character for about a minute before reverting to their stage persona. I never used to think anything about them when I saw them on TV, but after being in their company, I can tell you they are funny people.

When people I know want items to auction for charity, I'll try and help them out if I can. Our Glyn wanted some items for an auction, so I got some items signed at a charity match in Manchester. When I approached Rodney Marsh and asked him for his autograph, I thought he was an arse-hole because he looked at me as though I was the village idiot. Denis Irwin is another one. He was playing in the same match and I approached him before they went out, asking

Mel STERLAND

him if he'd sign something. He looked at me and said dismissively, "In a bit, after the game." His attitude really pissed me off, so I said, "Fuck you then, I don't want your autograph" and just walked off.

People send photos to me via Sheffield Wednesday or Leeds, asking me to sign and return them, but I don't bother because I know they just end up selling them on eBay. If the picture's any good, I usually keep it so that when someone in the pub asks me for a picture, I've got one to give to them. If I do sign a photo, I make sure that it's dedicated to someone, rather than just writing "Best Wishes" or whatever. So if you're reading this and thinking you can make a few quid out of me by sending some pictures for me to sign, don't bother!

I still attend Sheffield Wednesday matches on a regular basis. The people who welcome me at Hillsborough are the ones who are still there from my time at the club. There's a lady called Elaine who deals with the corporate guests and she's absolutely fantastic. Elaine's been there for years and her mother also worked at the club.

I've done some radio work in the past, summarising on matches. When I first had a go at it on *BBC Radio Sheffield*, I was very nervous. Some people are natural broadcasters and find it easy, but I found it difficult at first because I was wondering what I was allowed to say. I love to have a laugh and, believe it or not, I sometimes like to eff and blind! There are times when you want to swear when you're summarising, but you obviously can't do that on radio, so you have to bite your tongue.

I think you've got to speak your mind when you're a summariser, otherwise

Boozing, Betting & Brawling

it's a waste of time going on. I was summarising on a Sheffield Wednesday game for *BBC Radio Sheffield* on one occasion when I criticised Wednesday keeper Kevin Pressman following a poor performance. Kevin came up to me later and made it clear he wasn't happy about my comments. "Fucking hell, what are you doing, having a go at me?" he said.

"Hold on, you're getting paid x amount of pounds and you're supposed to save fucking shots and come for crosses," I said. "I'm getting paid a lot less than you and I'm on the radio to speak my mind and tell the truth about what I've seen."

"Well, there's no need for that."

"Oh, fuck off."

"Pressie" is a nice kid and he still speaks to me, but he can be miserable. I think he thought that because I knew him, I wouldn't say anything critical about his performance. But people are watching the games and if you don't tell the truth, they'll go away thinking, "What's he on about, him, has he watched the same game as me?" You can't sit on the fence and if a certain player doesn't like what I say, so what, they can bollocks!

One of the funniest times I had working as a co-commentator came when I was with *BBC Radio Sheffield* reporter Dave Burns at Southampton's old ground, The Dell. The Press Box there was very narrow so it was difficult to get into your seat. We were live on air as we watched a guy clambering along a ledge, trying to get to his seat, only to end up falling through a window! We were supposed to be looking ahead to the game but we couldn't talk for laughing.

Mel STERLAND

I think "Burnsy" had to hand back to the studio for a few minutes because we just couldn't stop laughing about what had happened.

I later did some work as a match-summariser for an independent station, *Radio Aire*, covering Leeds United games. The station provided commentary on all the Leeds games when they were in the Premiership, but that stopped when they were relegated.

I get invited to some Leeds games and it's always nice to go back. I went to Elland Road for the game against Forest in February 2008 and I was chatting about the old days with Paul Reaney when Ken Bates came into the room. I'd never met him before so Paul introduced him to me. Bates just took one look at me and said, "Fucking hell, you're a fat cunt now, aren't you?!" I just laughed because I didn't know what to say. I wanted to say, "You're a fat hairy bastard who looks like Father Christmas," but I didn't. That's the way he is; he thinks he can say what he wants. Apparently, when he met Reaney for the first time, he said, "I hate people who wear brown shoes."

When I was looking at the possibility of doing some media work, I went on a one-day training course at the *Press Association's* training headquarters in Howden with a number of other ex-players including Imre Varadi, Gordon Hill and Greg Fee. The late Danny Bergara was also there. Danny, who coached Sheffield United and managed Stockport, among others, was a great guy. He came from Uruguay and joined Sheffield United in the late 1970s when Harry Haslam was manager. At the start of the training course, we were asked to stand up individually and introduce ourselves. You had to say something along

Boozing, Betting & Brawling

the lines of: "I'm Mel Sterland, I played for Sheffield Wednesday, Glasgow Rangers, Leeds and England....." The introduction was supposed to only last a few minutes. Me, Imre, Gordon and Greg all did our introductions within that sort of time and then it was Danny's turn. He got up and started talking about his career in detail, going on and on. He told us who he'd played for and then listed the players he'd coached and explained how he could bend a ball. We were all sat there saying, "For fuck's sake Danny, we want to get this over and done with so we can get off home, fucking sit down." He must have been on his feet for half an hour before finally sitting down.

We were then handed packs of paper relating to the course before having a coffee break. We all put our packs down on the table, by the side of the coffee pot which Danny then picked up to pour himself a drink. He unscrewed the top and then as he started pouring the coffee into his cup, we were all watching him, sensing what was about to happen. Sure enough, the top came off pouring red-hot coffee all over the hand Danny was using to hold his cup, spilling it all over the paperwork.

"Fucking bastard!" he shouted in his pigeon-English as he shook the coffee off his scalded hand. We were all falling about laughing. In fact, I don't think I've ever laughed so much in my life. Not only had Danny wasted time with his long-winded speech, his cock-up with the coffee resulted in a further delay because we had to wait for some fresh paperwork to arrive because the packs had been ruined. I used to see Danny around Sheffield because he kept his home in the city until he died and he was a great character.

Mel STERLAND

My daughter Chantelle, who works in a secondary school in Sheffield, absolutely loves football and often goes to Sheffield Wednesday games with me. But my son Nathan, who works in loss prevention in a Sheffield department store, hates it. He's not bothered one bit about the game. I think he's only just found out who I played for and he's 21!

When I had a chance to buy the lease on a pub, which I'd agreed to take over with my brother Glyn, I had to raise some money to put in my share and selling my English and Scottish Championship medals was the easiest way to do it. I don't know how to work a computer so I had to ask someone to put them on eBay for me. He listed the First Division and Second Division Championship medals from my time at Leeds and the Scottish Premiership winner's medal I won at Rangers. Putting the medals up for auction attracted a lot of publicity, with stories in the national newspapers saying that I was selling them because I was skint. That's not the case though. Admittedly, I don't have as much money as I'd like to have, but the bills get paid and I'm not skint.

The medals were just in a cabinet and I didn't hesitate to sell them because I've got my memories. There was loads of interest, especially in the First Division medal I won at Leeds. There was a "Mrs Revie" who just missed out on that, going to about £6,500 before dropping out of the bidding. Whether that was Don Revie's widow or his son's missus, I don't know. A lad from Wolverhampton bought the Leeds medals. I received seven-and-a-half grand for the First Division medal and about five grand for the Second Division one. The Scottish medal raised two-and-a-half grand. I've also sold the European Championship winner's medal I won with the England Under-21s. When I look back, I don't regret selling the medals.

I kept my full England cap, along with my three "B" caps and seven Under-21 caps. They're for my grandson. He keeps putting them on and they look good on him.

I got offered five grand for my full England cap, but I wasn't tempted to sell.

As it turned out, after I raised my money and Glyn raised half of his money, the deal for the pub fell through when the guy selling the lease decided he didn't want to sell after all. I love pubs and it's fair to say that I spend quite a bit of time in them, but I couldn't take one on now due to my health problems.

Even though I've been retired for 16 years, I still get a lot of people coming up to me when I'm out to talk to me about my career. I don't mind it on the whole when people want to do that. It irritates me though when people who don't know anything about football, but think they do, come up and start spouting off. I either tell them to "fuck off" or I go elsewhere for a pint. I still do presentations for junior football teams. The kids are obviously too young to know who I am but their parents remember me playing.

People ask me whether I wish I'd done things differently in my life. "Do you wish you'd gone down another road?" they say. But I can honestly say that I wouldn't change a thing about my life. I'd swear that on a bible. I've loved every minute because it's been fantastic and exciting. After coming off a scruffy estate, I've won medals and played for my country. I've travelled the world and if it wasn't for football, I wouldn't have done that or had what I've had. I've also got a nice wife, two lovely kids and a grandson who means the world to me.

Okay, I might not have the big money and the large house anymore, but they can't take away your memories. I think that you just have to get on with what you've got and that's what I do. I've enjoyed myself and I don't regret anything, not a thing.

MEL STERLAND – CAREER RECORD

	League Apps/Goals	FA Cup Apps/Goals	League Cup Apps/Goals
SHEFFIELD WEDNESDAY	279/37	35/5	30/7
GLASGOW RANGERS	9/3	4/0 (Scottish Cup)	
LEEDS UNITED	114/16	10/1	13/1
TOTAL:	**402/56**	**49/6**	**43/8**

TOTAL APPS: 494

TOTAL GOALS: 70

DOMESTIC HONOURS:

Division One title: 1991/92

Division Two title: 1989/90

Scottish Premier Division title: 1988/89

INTERNATIONAL HONOURS (ENGLAND):

SENIOR: 1 cap/0 goals – v Saudi Arabia, 1988/89

'B': 2 caps/1 goal – v Malta, 1987/88 (1 goal); v Yugoslavia (sub) 1989/90

UNDER-21: 7 caps/3 goals – v Denmark, Hungary, France (twice), Italy, Spain (twice), all 1983/84. *1 goal v France, I goal (pen) v Italy, 1 goal v Spain.

EUROPEAN UNDER-21 CHAMPIONSHIP WINNERS' MEDAL, 1984